The Power of Legacy: Holistic Leadership for Lasting Impact

Dr. Jamika Bivens

Copyright © 2026 Dr. Jamika Bivens

All rights reserved. No part of this book may be reproduced or transmitted in any form or by any means without prior written permission of the publisher, except for brief quotations in reviews.

Published by Bivens Consulting Group

ISBN: 979-8-9944288-1-8

DEDICATION

To every leader who chooses people over ego,
purpose over applause,
and legacy over urgency—
this book is for you.

To my village—family, mentors, colleagues, and friends—
who saw leadership in me before I could name it for myself,
thank you for teaching me how to lead with heart and courage.

And to every young woman watching from the margins,
wondering if her voice belongs at the table—
pull up your seat.
You were born to lead.

– Jamika

CONTENTS

	Acknowledgments	vii
	Preface	viii
	Introduction	xiii
	Leadership Tools at a Glance	xvi
1	Leading with Wholeness	1
2	Visionary Leadership and Innovation	22
3	Strategic Thinking for Legacy-Minded Leaders	38
4	Communicating with Impact	58
5	Building Dynamic Teams	79
6	Coaching and Mentorship	97
7	Ethical Decision-Making	117
8	Character & Virtue	135
9	Leading Through Adversity & Renewal	151
10	The Power of Legacy and Lasting Impact	169

ACKNOWLEDGMENTS

This book would not exist without the wisdom, support, and faith of many.
To my family—thank you for grounding me, loving me, and reminding me that leadership starts at home. You taught me how to serve, how to speak truth, and how to rise.

To my mentors, colleagues, and the incredible professionals I've had the privilege of working alongside—thank you for sharpening my thinking and expanding my vision. You showed me that leadership isn't about titles; it's about presence, purpose, and people.

To my spiritual and community leaders, thank you for reminding me that every gift comes with responsibility. This work is as much a calling as it is a career.

And to every reader—thank you for showing up with humility, hunger, and hope. You are the reason this message matters. If this book planted one seed in you to lead with more conviction, more compassion, or more courage, then it has done its work.

With deep gratitude,
Jamika

PREFACE

I have always believed that leadership is about people, purpose, and principles. Long before I had a title or formal authority, I understood that the way we influence others, the way we build trust, and the way we live our values have the power to shape lives. Leadership is never just about outcomes; it is about impact. That conviction has guided me throughout my journey and is the heartbeat of this book.

For me, leadership has always been deeply personal. I did not set out to write about strategy or theory alone. I wrote because I have seen the difference between leadership that fades when circumstances change and leadership that leaves a mark long after the leader has stepped away. The difference is legacy. And legacy is built not by accident, but through daily choices, intentional practices, and values lived consistently.

My Journey into Leadership

I did not arrive at these insights overnight. They were shaped through years of leading people, building teams, mentoring future leaders, and navigating the challenges of organizational change. I have had the privilege of guiding leaders at every level — from those just beginning to step into influence to seasoned executives shaping entire organizations. Along the way, I discovered that success without substance is fragile. A leader may achieve impressive results in the short term, but if those results are not grounded in purpose, values, and people, they rarely last.

As I studied leadership formally and practiced it in real time, I realized how often traditional leadership models fall short. They emphasize performance metrics without addressing character. They train leaders to manage systems but not to nurture people. They focus on short-term goals while neglecting long-term vision. Over time, I became convinced that what leaders need most is not just another set of tools but a framework that integrates every part of who they are — their strategy, their ethics, their resilience, and their capacity to develop others.

That conviction shaped my own leadership journey. Whether mentoring an emerging leader, helping a team find its footing during a season of change, or guiding an organization through transitions, I found myself returning again and again to the same truth: leadership must be holistic. It must reach beyond surface-level performance and touch the deeper dimensions of people, purpose, and principles.

These lessons taught me that leadership cannot be reduced to a checklist or a role. It is lived, day by day, in the choices we make, the values we embody, and the people we invest in. Over time, I realized that my calling was not only to lead but to help others discover a framework for leadership that could be both deeply human and enduring.

Why I Wrote This Book

I wrote this book because I believe leadership must be reimagined. Too many leaders chase recognition, titles, or short-term victories, only to realize those pursuits leave them empty — and leave their people disillusioned. I wanted to offer something different: a way of leading that builds trust, inspires courage, and leaves an imprint that endures.

Holistic leadership is not about perfection. It is about integration. It is about leaders who understand that their influence extends beyond quarterly results, beyond the span of their careers, and even beyond their own lifetimes. It is about leading in such a way that the culture, values, and people you invest in continue to grow even after you are gone.

I have seen leaders struggle to balance competing demands — strategy with ethics, vision with daily execution, results with people development. Too often, they are told they must choose one or the other. But I believe the best leaders learn to hold them together. Holistic leadership provides a framework for doing just that.

This book is also born out of my own commitment to live what I teach. I hold a Doctor of Strategic Leadership, an MBA, and several professional certifications. These credentials gave me tools, but the fundamental transformation came from practicing leadership in the trenches — in conversations, decisions, and moments that tested values and resilience. I have spent years designing curriculum, facilitating leadership programs, and building training frameworks.

Yet the lessons that matter most have not come only from credentials. They have come from walking with real people through real challenges — seeing growth emerge from mentoring conversations, watching resilience build through adversity, and witnessing innovation take root when teams dare to imagine more.

What I Hope You Will Gain

This book is written as both a guide and a companion. You will find theory here, because leadership must be grounded in wisdom. You will find personal stories, because leadership is always lived in the real world. And you will find practical tools, because leadership must be practiced daily to have an impact.

My hope is that as you move through these pages, you will do more than gather knowledge. I hope you will reflect on your own journey, challenge yourself to grow, and commit to practicing leadership in ways that create transformation.

This book is not meant to sit on a shelf as theory. I hope that it becomes a trusted companion, a resource you return to in moments of decision, conflict, or vision casting. As you work through the pages, you will be challenged, encouraged, and equipped to lead with clarity and courage. Most importantly, you will be reminded that your leadership is never just about today — it is about the legacy you are shaping for tomorrow.

The Vision for This Book

This book offers a roadmap to holistic leadership by guiding readers through its essential dimensions. The chapters move in a deliberate progression, beginning with vision and self-awareness, then expanding into communication, character, team building, and the development of others. Along the way, the emphasis remains on ethical decision-making, resilience in adversity, and the courage to innovate for the future. Each chapter provides both principles and practical steps, so that by the conclusion, readers will not only understand holistic leadership in theory but also possess a framework for living it in practice and leaving a lasting legacy.

A Word to the Reader

As you read this book, I want you to know that you are not alone on this journey. Leadership is demanding, and there will be moments when you feel the weight of responsibility. There will also be moments of profound joy when you see growth in the people you lead and realize the difference your presence makes.

My encouragement to you is this: embrace the challenge. Do the inner work as well as the outer work. Choose integrity when compromise feels easier. Dare to cast vision when others can only see obstacles. Invest in people even when it takes time and patience. And never forget that the legacy you leave will not be measured only by results but by the lives you've touched and the values you've lived.

This book is my invitation to you — to step into leadership that is holistic, transformational, and enduring. If you are willing, the journey that follows will equip you to build something greater than yourself.

With you on the journey,
Jamika

INTRODUCTION

Leadership today faces significant challenges. While there is no shortage of individuals in positions of authority, too often leadership has become narrowly defined by short-term outcomes, metrics, and appearances. In many settings, success is measured by titles earned, influence accumulated, or recognition gained. Yet these measures alone rarely capture the depth of what leadership is meant to be.

The consequences are easy to recognize: organizations may achieve quarterly results but struggle with trust. Leaders may build recognizable brands but overlook the growth of their people. Teams may hit targets but remain uncertain of a greater purpose. Leadership risks becoming transactional — focused only on immediate gains — rather than transformational, invested in what will endure.

This is the challenge of our time: leadership that reacts to the moment rather than shaping the future, that emphasizes activity over impact, and that prizes visibility more than vision. History reminds us that while contexts change, the defining distinction remains constant: leadership rooted in self-interest fades, while leadership rooted in legacy endures.

The Gap

Why does this gap exist? Many leaders are encouraged to focus on measures of success that can be quickly observed — profitability, recognition, or efficiency. These have value, but when they become the only focus, something important is lost. Leadership at its best is not only about results, but about shaping people, cultures, and futures that outlast any single role or season.

Authority without trust proves hollow. Metrics without meaning rarely inspire hearts. Expedience without ethics may produce wins that cannot be sustained. In contrast, legacy provides an anchor. It grounds leadership in values and purpose, ensuring that influence lasts beyond immediate circumstances.

In today's world, organizations, communities, and families alike need leaders who balance results with responsibility, who look beyond the present moment to invest in what will matter most tomorrow.

The Call to Holistic Leadership

This book responds to that need. Holistic leadership is leadership that integrates every dimension of who we are — strategy, character, communication, resilience, and vision — into a coherent whole. It is not about excelling in one area while neglecting others; it is about leading from a place of integration, where personal values, organizational purpose, and people development converge.

Holistic leadership is as much about process as it is about outcomes. It is about how goals are pursued, not just what is achieved. It is about creating leaders, not only gaining followers. It is about shaping organizations, communities, and cultures through the consistency of how we lead in meetings, decisions, and moments of influence.

At its core, holistic leadership is guided by a central question: *What will my leadership leave behind?*

What Legacy Really Means

Legacy is more than reputation or recognition, though it may include both. Legacy is influence that continues — values lived with such clarity and consistency that others carry them forward. It is the culture formed through daily decisions, the investment made in people, and the impact that multiplies long after a leader has moved on.

A leader's legacy is not defined on the day they receive their title or on the day they step down. It is described in the thousands of choices in between — the words spoken in meetings, the courage shown in crises, the consistency modeled in daily life.

Legacy is the most accurate measure of leadership.

A Personal Invitation

As you begin this journey, I want to invite you into a different posture of leadership. Not one that chases titles, accolades, or short-term gains, but one that embraces the deeper call to build something that lasts.

I know what it feels like to face pressure to compromise, to wonder if vision will ever take root, to lead through fatigue and conflict. I also know the joy of watching people grow, of seeing values lived out in culture, and of realizing that what you invested in continues even after you step away. That is the reward of legacy-minded leadership — not fleeting applause, but lasting transformation.

This book is written for leaders at every level: emerging leaders who want to start strong, seasoned leaders who want to lead with integrity, and those in between who want to anchor their leadership in something greater than themselves.

Wherever you find yourself, you hold within your hands the opportunity to shape your legacy. And that begins not in the distant future, but here, in this moment, with the choices you make today.

Your Legacy Starts Now

This book is an invitation to lead with vision, integrity, and courage — to embrace holistic leadership that transforms both people and purpose. As you read, reflect, and apply what follows, remember that legacy is not something you stumble into at the end of your career. It is something you build daily, through presence, choices, and values lived consistently.

I invite you to read slowly, reflect deeply, and apply boldly — because the world needs leaders who are willing to do the inner work required for lasting change.

The journey begins here. Your legacy starts now.

LEADERSHIP TOOLS AT A GLANCE

Chapter	Tool / Framework	Purpose in Leadership
Chapter 1 – Strategic Vision	Strategic Visioning Practices	Anchor today's actions in a compelling, long-term direction.
Chapter 2 – Self-Awareness	Johari Window	Reveal blind spots by inviting trusted feedback.
	DiSC Assessment	Understand behavioral tendencies and build a shared team language.
	Reflective Journaling	Clarify decisions, emotions, and lessons through consistent writing.
	360-Degree Feedback	Gain full-circle insights from supervisors, peers, and direct reports.
	Predictive Index / Behavioral Assessments	Identify natural drives that shape work and relationships.
	Mindfulness Practices	Build presence, regulate emotions, and respond intentionally.
Chapter 3 – Communication	SBI Feedback Model	Give feedback with clarity and respect (Situation, Behavior, Impact).
	Nonviolent Communication (NVC)	Transform conflict into constructive dialogue.
	Mindfulness Practices (applied to communication)	Stay present and choose intentional responses in conversation.

Chapter	Tool / Framework	Purpose in Leadership
Chapter 4 – Character & Virtue	Integrity Ledger	Align commitments with actions through weekly accountability.
Chapter 5 – Teams	Psychological Safety Practices	Create environments where every voice is safe to contribute.
	Strengths-Based Practices	Assign roles that leverage individual talents for team resilience.
Chapter 6 – Coaching & Mentorship	GROW Model	Structure coaching conversations to empower growth.
	Hybrid Matching	Blend structure with mentee choice for stronger mentorship.
Chapter 7 – Ethics & Moral Courage	Ethical Decision Filters	Test choices against transparency, impact, values, and legacy.
Chapter 8 – Resilience & Renewal	Energy Portfolio	Sustain performance by balancing physical, emotional, mental, and spiritual energy.
Chapter 9 – Visionary Innovation	Design Thinking	Innovate through empathy, experimentation, and rapid learning.
Chapter 10 – Legacy	Legacy Map	Track quarterly: values upheld, people invested in, and impact that endures.

1 LEADING WITH WHOLENESS

If vision is the compass of leadership, then self-awareness is the anchor. Without it, leaders drift into blind spots and repeat patterns that erode trust. With it, they build authenticity, credibility, and influence that lasts.

Leadership is not only about what we accomplish but also about *who we are while accomplishing it*. A leader can drive performance but lose credibility if their actions betray their words. They can inspire others with vision, but erode trust if their character lacks consistency. To lead with wholeness is to integrate values, character, behavior, and purpose into a seamless whole. Wholeness means that the public leader and the private individual are not at odds. It means there is no contradiction between what is promised and what is delivered, between what is preached and what is practiced.

When leaders are fragmented—when their actions drift from their values—followers sense it. Trust weakens. Cynicism grows. Wholeness, by contrast, produces alignment. It creates confidence that a leader can be relied upon, that their decisions will not waver under pressure, and that their influence is worth following. Leading with wholeness is essential for building the kind of legacy that endures.

If self-awareness anchors the leader, wholeness shapes the vessel. To understand what we are anchoring, we first need a clear picture of holistic leadership. We'll define it plainly, anchor it in values, and then translate it into a practice you can repeat.

Defining Holistic Leadership

Holistic leadership is more than a style or technique. It is a philosophy that integrates the mind, heart, and spirit of leadership into a unified approach. Where some leaders are content to drive performance metrics alone, holistic leaders recognize that lasting impact flows from cultivating people, culture, and values. Holistic leadership asks: *How can I serve not just the organization's goals, but the growth and flourishing of those I lead?*

Unlike transactional leadership, which emphasizes exchange (rewards for tasks completed), holistic leadership emphasizes transformation. The holistic leader's measure of success is not simply profit margins or efficiency ratios, but whether the people under their care are developing into stronger, wiser, and more empowered leaders themselves.

Key values of holistic leadership include:
- **Integrity:** Acting consistently with values, even when it is costly.
- **Accountability:** Taking responsibility for both successes and failures.
- **Compassion:** Caring for people as whole beings, not just employees.
- **Respect:** Recognizing dignity across differences.
- **Servanthood:** Placing the needs of others before personal ambition.

Holistic leadership is deeply connected to the concept of **servant leadership**. Robert Greenleaf described servant leaders as those who begin with the natural desire to serve first, and then lead as an extension of that service. Holistic leadership builds upon this premise by weaving in the whole dimension of human development—emotional, intellectual, social, and ethical. It requires leaders to see followers not merely as laborers or performers, but as future leaders in their own right.

A philosophy becomes real only when it touches culture. Here is why wholeness isn't optional—why it shows up in trust, behavior, and long-term impact. Philosophy alone doesn't change culture; leaders do.

Why Wholeness Matters

In leadership, cracks in character eventually become chasms in culture. A leader who speaks about integrity but cuts corners sets a precedent that others will follow. A leader who preaches inclusion but dismisses dissent creates a climate of fear. A leader who values results above all else may succeed in the short term but leaves behind a trail of disillusionment.

Wholeness matters because leadership is contagious. People may listen to what leaders say, but they replicate what leaders do. If there is a gap between words and actions, the gap spreads. Over time, the culture mirrors the inconsistency of its leaders.

This is why legacy-minded leaders commit to wholeness. They understand that the true measure of leadership is not only outcomes achieved but also values upheld. A legacy is not built by a list of accomplishments alone. It is built by a life lived with integrity.

Principle must become practice. The Nine Steps of Holistic Leadership translate the idea of wholeness into daily leadership habits. To move from intention to rhythm, we'll use a simple cycle you can run again and again.

The Nine Steps of Holistic Leadership™

Wholeness in leadership is not a vague ideal. It can be cultivated through intentional practice. The Nine Steps of Holistic Leadership (HL9™) provide a framework for living and leading with alignment. These steps form a cycle that leaders return to repeatedly as circumstances evolve.

1. **Clarify Purpose & Values:** Identify what matters most. Define the non-negotiables that guide decisions.
2. **Scan the Environment:** Study both internal strengths and external realities using tools like SWOT and PESTLE.
3. **Craft the Vision:** Paint a picture of the future that aligns with purpose and values.
4. **Set Strategic Priorities:** Choose a small set of must-win goals and define clear metrics for success.
5. **Align People & Structure:** Organize teams, roles, and systems so they reinforce the vision and support inclusion.

6. **Communicate & Build Trust:** Speak consistently and transparently. Establish rhythms that reduce anxiety.
7. **Develop Self & Emotional Intelligence:** Surface blind spots, regulate emotions, and model authenticity.
8. **Develop Others:** Invest in mentoring, coaching, and building the leadership pipeline.
9. **Institutionalize Legacy:** Codify practices, document lessons, and embed values into culture.

The power is in the repeat: run the cycle, learn, and run it again.

How to Use the Nine Steps

The Nine Steps are not linear boxes to check off. They are a cycle. For example, after aligning people and structure (Step 5), a leader may discover blind spots requiring more personal development (Step 7). Or after institutionalizing legacy (Step 9), new external realities may prompt another environmental scan (Step 2). Leaders return to the cycle again and again, refining clarity, strengthening culture, and expanding impact.

By practicing these steps consistently, leaders anchor their wholeness in daily rhythms rather than occasional inspiration. Every cycle begins at the center: purpose and values. Without them, direction fractures; with them, decisions align. Let's walk the cycle once, step by step, beginning where all durable leadership begins—purpose and values.

Step 1: Clarify Purpose and Values — The Foundation of Wholeness

Leading with wholeness begins by clarifying purpose and values. Without clarity, leaders drift, chasing opportunities that may undermine integrity. With clarity, leaders stand firm, even in turbulence.

I recall early in my career when I was faced with a choice between taking on a project that promised quick results but compromised our values, or declining it and risking criticism for being "too idealistic." The easy path was tempting. But I remembered the bigger picture—we were not just building short-term wins, we were shaping a culture. Saying no was costly in the moment, but it preserved credibility. Years later, those same values became the reason people trusted me with greater responsibility. Clarity names the non-negotiables; now scan the landscape that will test them.

Tool in Practice — The Integrity Ledger™: Write down every promise or commitment made, however small, and track whether it is fulfilled. At week's end, review and share openly with your team. This practice turns abstract values into visible accountability.

Purpose and values ensure that decisions today strengthen rather than weaken the foundation tomorrow. Clarity must meet reality. Once the purpose is firm, leaders scan the landscape to understand what helps or hinders that purpose.

Step 2: Scan the Environment

Clarifying purpose is not enough. Leaders must continually scan the environment to see how external trends and internal realities affect their ability to lead with wholeness.

Leaders cannot lead with clarity if they only look inward. To make sound decisions, they must understand both the internal dynamics of their teams and the external forces shaping their environment. Two structured tools help leaders discipline their thinking and avoid blind spots: **SWOT Analysis** and **PESTLE Analysis**. Used together, these tools give leaders a 360-degree view of where they stand, what challenges they face, and what opportunities lie ahead. We start inside-out with a clear inventory of what we do well, where we struggle, and what's on the horizon.

Tool in Practice — SWOT Analysis

A **SWOT Analysis** helps leaders identify **strengths, weaknesses, opportunities, and threats**. It is deceptively simple, but when practiced with honesty and rigor, it reveals patterns that leaders might otherwise overlook.

- **Strengths** highlight what the team or organization does well—its distinctive capabilities, values, and cultural assets.
- **Weaknesses** force leaders to name the internal gaps that could undermine progress.
- **Opportunities** uncover emerging trends, partnerships, or market shifts that could be leveraged.
- **Threats** identify risks or external pressures that could derail the mission.

Application: Schedule a quarterly SWOT session with your team. Divide a whiteboard or virtual board into four quadrants. Invite people to name one observation for each category. Resist the urge to debate or justify. The goal is not perfection—it is perspective. Once ideas are listed, ask: *Which strengths can we double down on? Which weaknesses must we address now? Which opportunities should we pursue? Which threats require contingency planning?*

Personal Example: Early in my leadership career, I facilitated a SWOT analysis for a department that had just experienced significant turnover. In the "strengths" quadrant, the team named their loyalty to one another and their deep industry knowledge. Under "weaknesses," they admitted communication silos that were slowing decision-making. "Opportunities" included the chance to redesign workflows with new technology, and "threats" included competition from firms already ahead in digital adoption. That one exercise shifted the narrative. Instead of feeling defeated by turnover, the team saw that their strengths positioned them to seize opportunities—if they addressed weaknesses directly.

While a SWOT analysis surfaces near-field dynamics, a PESTLE analysis widens the lens to the broader forces we cannot control but must understand.

Tool in Practice — PESTLE Analysis

While SWOT focuses on the internal organization and immediate external factors, a **PESTLE Analysis** pushes leaders to scan the broader environment—**Political, Economic, Social, Technological, Legal, and Environmental** trends. This tool forces leaders to step back and ask: *What is changing around us that we cannot control, but must understand?*

- **Political:** Policy changes, regulations, and government stability.
- **Economic:** Inflation, employment trends, and global markets.
- **Social:** Demographic shifts, cultural expectations, and consumer behavior.
- **Technological:** Innovations, digital disruption, and new platforms.
- **Legal:** Compliance requirements, liability risks, and evolving laws.
- **Environmental:** Sustainability, climate concerns, and

resource availability.

Application: Conduct a PESTLE scan twice a year. Assign each category to a small group or individual to research. Ask them to return with the top two or three trends that could affect your organization or team. Then, as a group, discuss: *Which of these trends present risks? Which present opportunities? How should we adapt?*

Personal Example: In one organization I served, a PESTLE revealed a technological disruption we hadn't accounted for—competitors were adopting automation tools that could drastically reduce operating costs. At first, this felt like a threat. But because we caught it early, we reframed it as an opportunity. We invested in training staff to work alongside automation rather than be displaced by it. As a result, we not only stayed competitive but positioned ourselves as an employer that cared about developing people rather than replacing them.

Why It Matters
SWOT and PESTLE aren't forms to fill; they're habits of awareness that widen perspective and steady decisions. They are about cultivating habits of awareness. They help leaders prevent tunnel vision and resist the temptation to rely on gut instinct alone. By combining the two, leaders see both the **inside-out** view (their own strengths and weaknesses) and the **outside-in** view (environmental forces they must adapt to).

The result is strategic clarity. Leaders can anticipate shifts, prepare contingencies, and seize opportunities without compromising their values. In a world with volatility, uncertainty, complexity, and ambiguity (VUCA), this discipline separates leaders who merely react from those who proactively build legacy. Insight needs direction. With context in hand, leaders craft a vision that names where we are going and why it matters. With context clarified, name a future worth moving toward.

Step 3: Craft the Vision

With clarity of purpose and awareness of context, leaders must craft a vision. Vision is not just a slogan on a wall—it is a vivid, compelling picture of the future that motivates people to move forward. Effective vision statements answer: *Where are we going? Why does it matter?*

Example: "In the next decade, our organization will expand into 10 new markets while investing in community programs that strengthen education and financial literacy."

Now we translate intention into a few must-win goals. Vision inspires; priorities mobilize.

Step 4: Set Strategic Priorities

Vision without execution dies in abstraction. This step turns vision into a manageable set of must-win priorities.

- Choose no more than 3–5 strategic priorities at a time.
- Define clear metrics of success (KPIs, milestones, cultural indicators).
- Make tradeoffs: say no to initiatives that don't serve the vision.

Priorities falter without the right architecture. People, roles, and systems must reinforce where we are headed. Priorities only stick when the org design supports them.

Step 5: Align People and Structure

Even the best strategy fails without the right people and systems in place. Leaders must design roles, teams, and processes that reinforce the vision.

This means:

- Hiring and promoting based on values and skills, not just technical expertise.
- Designing inclusive structures where diverse voices are represented.
- Eliminating silos that create competition instead of collaboration.

Even the best design will stall without clear, predictable communication.

Step 6: Communicate and Build Trust

Communication is the glue of holistic leadership. Without clear, consistent communication, even strong teams unravel.

- Share vision and priorities often until they become embedded in culture.
- Establish communication rhythms—weekly updates, town halls, or feedback sessions.
- Be transparent about both successes and setbacks.

Structures can hold a plan; only character can hold pressure. Developing self and growing emotional intelligence keeps leadership steady. Communication builds clarity; character sustains it—beginning with emotional intelligence.

Step 7: Develop Self and Emotional Intelligence (EQ)

Wholeness in leadership requires self-awareness. Leaders who do not know their blind spots or cannot regulate their emotions erode trust quickly. Wholeness multiplies when it's shared. The next move is to build leaders who will build leaders. We'll deepen EQ shortly; for now, remember that unexamined triggers become unintentional behaviors. Whole leaders make whole teams.

Step 8: Develop Others

Holistic leaders multiply leadership by mentoring, coaching, and preparing others to lead. Legacy is not what you accomplish alone but what you enable others to achieve.

Practical applications:
- Create formal mentorship programs.
- Provide coaching moments in everyday conversations.
- Invest in leadership pipelines that reflect diversity, equity, and inclusion.

Momentum becomes memory when we codify it. Institutionalizing legacy preserves hard-won gains beyond any one leader. To make progress durable, capture it in culture.

Step 9: Institutionalize Legacy
The final step is embedding practices, values, and lessons into the organization so they outlast the individual leader.

This can be done by:
- Codifying leadership practices into handbooks, rituals, and training.
- Documenting lessons learned after major initiatives.
- Creating "legacy summaries" each quarter—highlighting values upheld, people developed, and systems improved.

Across every step, one force binds wholeness together: emotional intelligence. It is the inner skill that shapes every outer practice.

Emotional Intelligence: The Heart of Holistic Leadership
In the 1990s, psychologists John Mayer and Peter Salovey introduced the concept of **emotional intelligence (EQ)**, later popularized by Daniel Goleman. Emotional intelligence refers to the ability to recognize, understand, and manage one's own emotions, and to recognize and influence the emotions of others. In leadership contexts, EQ is not a "nice to have"—it is a core competency that often determines effectiveness more than technical skill or IQ.

Leading from the Inside Out
EQ turns inner clarity into outer consistency—here's a simple way to practice it in real time. A leader cannot project integrity externally if they are fragmented internally. This is why emotional intelligence (EQ) is central to leading with wholeness.

Emotional intelligence involves:
- **Self-awareness:** Recognizing your own emotions.
- **Self-regulation:** Managing impulses and reactions.
- **Empathy:** Understanding the emotions of others.
- **Social skill:** Building healthy, productive relationships.

One practical tool is the **Pause–Name–Choose** method. When emotions run high, leaders pause, name the feeling honestly, and then choose a response aligned with values. This simple discipline prevents emotional reactions from undermining trust.

In my own practice, I have found that pausing for just 10 seconds before responding in a heated moment can shift the entire tone of a conversation. It allows me to lead from values rather than from frustration. Teams notice this consistency and trust that leadership decisions are steady.

The Five Dimensions of EQ

1. **Self-Awareness** – The ability to recognize one's own emotions, triggers, and behavioral tendencies. Self-aware leaders know how their moods influence their decision-making.
2. **Self-Regulation** – The discipline to control impulses, remain calm under stress, and avoid destructive reactions.
3. **Motivation** – A drive that transcends external rewards; leaders motivated by values and purpose inspire greater commitment from their teams.
4. **Empathy** – The ability to perceive and respond to the emotions of others, creating trust and rapport.
5. **Social Skills** – The capacity to build relationships, resolve conflict, and influence people positively.

Emotional intelligence is not a soft skill; it is a core leadership competency. Teams may forgive occasional mistakes in judgment, but they rarely forgive leaders who lack empathy or self-control. High-EQ leaders are better decision-makers, stronger communicators, and more trusted by their followers. Conversely, leaders who lack EQ may possess intelligence and strategy but alienate those they lead, undermining their impact.

Self-awareness grows when we face what we cannot see. That's why the next frontier is confronting blind spots.

Blind Spots: The Leadership Danger Zone

Even the most self-aware leaders possess blind spots—areas where they lack insight into their behavior, impact, or assumptions. Blind spots are dangerous precisely because leaders are unaware of them, even as others clearly see their effects.

Psychologists describe the Johari Window as a helpful framework for understanding blind spots. It divides awareness into four quadrants and acts like a mirror for leaders.

- **Open Area:** Known to self and others.
- **Hidden Area:** Known to self, not to others.
- **Blind Area:** Unknown to self, known to others.
- **Unknown Area:** Unknown to self and others.

It maps what is known to you, what others see in you, and the blind spots you cannot yet see. Inviting trusted colleagues to share what they observe shrinks those blind spots and builds trust. For example, a colleague might say, *"You believe you are approachable, but I hesitate to speak up."* Though uncomfortable, that insight is invaluable. Practiced regularly, this tool reinforces humility, accountability, and legacy-minded leadership by leaving a culture of openness.

Blind spots exist in the "Blind Area"—behaviors or attitudes visible to others but invisible to the leader. Effective leaders intentionally shrink this area by seeking feedback and cultivating humility. Naming blind spots is courageous; shrinking them is disciplined. These tools turn feedback into growth.

Tools for Leading with Wholeness
Blind Spot Assessments

Wholeness requires self-awareness, and self-awareness requires the courage to confront blind spots. Blind spots are not weaknesses we already know about; they are the behaviors, habits, or assumptions that everyone else sees but we do not. Left unexamined, blind spots damage credibility, relationships, and results.

Leaders cannot grow what they refuse to see. That is why **Blind Spot Assessments** are essential. They provide the mirror we cannot hold up for ourselves.

How to Use Blind Spot Assessments
1. **Invite honest feedback.** Use tools like 360-degree reviews, anonymous surveys, or structured conversations with colleagues.
2. **Compare perceptions.** Contrast how you see yourself with how others see you. Look for gaps that reveal blind spots.
3. **Identify one focus area per quarter.** Instead of trying to fix everything, choose one pattern to address.
4. **Create a practice plan.** Develop small habits to shift the blind spot into awareness.
5. **Review progress regularly.** Return to the same colleagues and ask, "Have you noticed improvement in this area?"

Why It Works

Blind Spot Assessments build humility. They demonstrate that leaders are willing to be vulnerable, to listen, and to change. Over time, this willingness builds credibility and encourages others to do the same.

A Personal Example

When I first stepped into a leadership role, I believed I was an excellent communicator. I gave detailed instructions, summarized action items, and checked for understanding. Yet, through a blind spot assessment, I learned that while I spoke clearly, I rarely paused to listen. Team members felt I was rushing them, more focused on moving forward than hearing their ideas.

That feedback stung, but it was invaluable. I began practicing intentional pauses, asking open-ended questions, and leaving space for silence. Over time, people noticed the difference. Meetings became more collaborative, and trust deepened. Without the assessment, I might have never discovered that blind spot, and my leadership would have been capped by my own assumptions.

Beyond general feedback, shared language accelerates team understanding. DiSC offers a practical vocabulary for collaboration.

DiSC and Beyond: The DiSC assessment reveals whether you lean toward Dominance, Influence, Steadiness, or Conscientiousness. It is not just a personality profile—it highlights how you naturally approach conflict, decision-making, and collaboration. By sharing your DiSC style with your team and learning theirs, you remove guesswork and create a common language for teamwork. Over time, this builds trust and reduces friction.

The DiSC assessment provides a shared language for how leaders and teams naturally operate.

- **Dominance (D):** Direct, results-oriented, assertive.
- **Influence (I):** Outgoing, persuasive, enthusiastic.
- **Steadiness (S):** Patient, cooperative, dependable.
- **Conscientiousness (C):** Analytical, precise, systematic.

Each style has strengths and overextensions. High-D leaders may drive results but risk insensitivity. High-I leaders may inspire enthusiasm but miss details. High-S leaders provide stability but resist change. High-C leaders ensure accuracy but may stall decisions.

To round out the toolkit, leaders add structured perspectives and guided reflection. Shared language reduces friction; shared habits sustain growth.

Other tools include:
- **360-Degree Feedback:** Inviting anonymous input from peers, subordinates, and supervisors.
- **Executive Coaching:** Structured relationships focused on reflection and growth.
- **Mindfulness Practices:** Techniques for cultivating presence and emotional regulation.

Values influence nothing until they are visible. Mapping values to behaviors makes culture observable—and coachable. Values only shape culture when they're visible in daily behavior.

Values-to-Behavior Mapping

Values often fail not because they are wrong but because they remain abstract. Employees hear words like "respect," "excellence," or "collaboration," but do not see how those values translate into daily work. **Values-to-Behavior Mapping** solves this gap by turning ideals into actions.

How to Use Values-to-Behavior Mapping
1. **List your core values.** Choose three to five values that matter most to you or your team.
2. **Identify behaviors.** For each value, define specific actions that bring it to life.
    - *Value: Respect → Behavior: Begin every meeting by hearing from each person in the room.*
    - *Value: Accountability → Behavior: End projects with a debrief where everyone names one thing they could have done better.*
3. **Integrate into routines.** Embed these behaviors into meetings, performance reviews, and recognition systems.
4. **Measure and reward.** Celebrate behaviors that embody values as much as outcomes.

Why It Works

Values become powerful only when they are observable. By linking values to behaviors, leaders remove ambiguity. Everyone knows what is expected, and culture shifts from abstract ideals to daily practice.

A Personal Example

In one department I led, we identified *collaboration* as a core value. At first, it felt aspirational. People agreed it was important, but it wasn't visible in meetings. We mapped it to a simple behavior: "No meeting ends without each member contributing at least one idea or update."

At first, it felt forced. But over the weeks, quieter voices began sharing, and insights surfaced that we would have otherwise missed. Collaboration moved from a word on the wall to a habit in the room. Eventually, team members began initiating collaboration outside of meetings as well. The value became a lived reality. Alongside assessments, reflective practices keep leaders honest over time. With shared language and visible behaviors in place, deepen the practice through regular reflection.

Practical Frameworks for Self-Awareness

Reflective Journaling: Reflective journaling is not simply writing for writing's sake; it is a disciplined pause for leaders to process their choices and emotions. By recording daily or weekly reflections on decisions made, lessons learned, and feelings experienced, leaders create a mirror of growth over time. A journal reveals patterns—recurring frustrations, moments of breakthrough, or habits that shape influence. Leaders who journal with intention gain clarity on their values and strengthen their capacity for self-correction. Over months and years, these written reflections become a record of integrity and wisdom, a personal archive of the legacy being built.

360-Degree Feedback provides a full-circle perspective from supervisors, peers, and direct reports.

Behavioral Assessments: Behavioral assessments such as the Predictive Index reveal the natural drives that shape how leaders approach work, relationships, and conflict. These tools are not boxes to confine people but maps that explain why certain behaviors come easily and others demand energy. For example, a leader with a high drive for dominance may excel at decisive calls but need to practice patience in consensus-building. By knowing these tendencies, leaders can design complementary teams, anticipate stress points, and stretch themselves beyond instinctive patterns. The ultimate value lies not in the profile itself but in how it equips a leader to lead intentionally and to multiply impact with balance.

Mindfulness Practices: Mindfulness is the practice of presence—pausing before reacting, noticing emotional triggers, and choosing responses rather than defaulting to impulses. For leaders, mindfulness is less about emptying the mind and more about training attention. A mindful leader can recognize when frustration is rising in a meeting and choose calm curiosity instead of a sharp reaction. Over time, mindfulness strengthens emotional intelligence, reduces reactive errors, and models steadiness for the team. In moments of crisis, mindful leaders are remembered not for panic but for composure. That legacy of steadiness becomes part of the culture they leave behind. Personal disciplines become cultural norms when leaders go first—publicly and consistently.

Building Wholeness into Culture

At one point in my leadership journey, I inherited a team that had experienced high turnover. Morale was low, and people did not trust leadership. Promises had been made and broken too many times. My first step was not to impose new initiatives but to rebuild trust.

I began keeping an Integrity Ledger™—not just privately but publicly. I shared my commitments each week with the team and reviewed them the following week. At first, there was skepticism. People waited to see if I would actually follow through. Over time, as promises consistently matched actions, trust slowly rebuilt. Team members began mirroring the practice themselves. Eventually, we created a culture where commitments were tracked and celebrated collectively.

This experience taught me that wholeness scales. It begins with a leader's choices but spreads until it shapes the identity of the entire team. Culture breathes through communication. Rhythm makes clarity predictable and trust repeatable. Once trust begins to rebuild, sustain it with cadence.

Communication as the Glue of Wholeness

Wholeness requires not only personal integrity but also consistent communication. Followers cannot trust what they do not understand. Leaders must communicate values and priorities repeatedly and transparently.

I established rhythms like:
- **Mission Mondays** to reconnect work to purpose.
- **Mid-Week Metrics** to check progress and adjust.
- **Friday Reflections** to celebrate learning and name challenges.

These routines created predictability. People knew when clarity was coming, which reduced anxiety. More importantly, they reinforced that words and actions were connected. Strategy was not hidden; it was shared openly. It's equally important to name the opposite: what happens when words and actions part ways. It's just as important to name the cost when leaders separate words from actions.

The Cost of Fragmented Leadership

It is worth naming the opposite of wholeness. Fragmented leadership erodes culture. When leaders act inconsistently, followers disengage. When values are compromised for expedience, trust evaporates. When personal blind spots are ignored, credibility fractures.

I once worked with a leader who would make bold commitments in public but rarely delivered in private. At first, the team gave grace. But over time, the gap between words and actions became too wide. Trust collapsed, and turnover followed. The lesson was clear: fragmentation is unsustainable.

This is why wholeness is not optional. It is the very foundation of leadership that lasts. What we value, we measure. Wholeness shows up in numbers as well as narratives. What we value, we also measure.

Measuring Wholeness

Wholeness can be measured. It shows up in metrics like:
- **Trust scores** in employee surveys.
- **Turnover rates** as a reflection of culture.
- **Engagement levels** in meetings and initiatives.
- **Feedback consistency** from 360 assessments.

Leaders who lead with wholeness consistently see higher engagement, stronger retention, and more resilient teams. With the why and how in place, here are simple daily practices that compound over time. Metrics guide attention; habits drive change.

Practical Steps for Holistic Leaders

Holistic leadership is not abstract—it requires daily practices.
1. **Build Feedback Loops:** Create safe channels for employees to speak truth without fear.
2. **Develop Accountability Partners:** Trusted colleagues who point out blind spots.
3. **Practice Reflection:** Journaling, prayer, or meditation to process emotions and decisions.
4. **Lead with Empathy:** Ask in every decision, "How will this affect people?"
5. **Model Vulnerability:** Admit mistakes openly to normalize growth.

When leaders normalize feedback, embrace EQ, and address blind spots, they build cultures of trust and resilience. Good intentions still drift. These common traps—and their counter-moves—keep growth on track. Even good intentions drift—watch for these common traps.

Pitfalls & Best Practices
Pitfall 1: Confusing Self-Awareness with Self-Criticism
- Example: Dwelling on mistakes and labeling yourself as a "bad leader."
- Best Practice: Use reflection to grow, not to shame.

Pitfall 2: Assuming Others See You as You See Yourself
- Example: Believing you're approachable when your team finds you intimidating.
- Best Practice: Invite feedback regularly to reveal blind spots.

Pitfall 3: Collecting Feedback Without Acting on It
- Example: Asking for feedback but never changing behavior.
- Best Practice: Show growth by applying insights and letting others see the difference.

Pitfall 4: Avoiding Emotions in Leadership
- Example: Believing emotions don't belong at work and ignoring your own triggers.
- Best Practice: Recognize emotions as signals; respond with intentionality.

Pitfall 5: Treating EI as Optional
- Example: Focusing only on technical skills while neglecting empathy.
- Best Practice: Treat emotional intelligence as central to trust and influence.

Reflection cements learning. Use these questions to convert insight into action. Turn insights into action with a few focused questions.

Reflective Questions:
1. How self-aware are you in high-stakes situations?
2. What feedback have you resisted, and why?
3. How do you respond when blind spots are revealed?
4. How do you integrate empathy into daily decision-making?

Journaling Prompts
- Write about a time you misunderstood how others perceived your leadership. What did you learn?
- Begin mapping your values to specific behaviors.
- Reflect on one piece of feedback you've received that changed the way you lead.

90-Day Self-Awareness Growth Plan

Month 1 – Awareness
- Begin reflective journaling 2–3 times a week.
- Ask one trusted peer: *"What is one strength and one blind spot you see in me?"*

Month 2 – Feedback
- Collect informal 360-degree feedback from at least 3 colleagues.
- Compare your self-perception with others' input.

Month 3 – Practice
- Identify one emotional trigger and practice pausing before responding.
- Share with your team one area you're working to improve, modeling humility.

In the end, legacy reflects presence. The way we show up—day after day—becomes the story others will tell.

Closing Encouragement

Practice compounds; consistency becomes character. Self-awareness is not only about personal growth; it is about shaping the kind of presence people will remember. Leaders who know themselves deeply lead others with authenticity — and authenticity is the seed of legacy.

Leading with wholeness is not perfection—it is consistency. It is the daily practice of aligning who you are with what you do. It is the courage to let your values, character, and commitments speak louder than your title.

Every decision, every promise, every conversation is either building or eroding trust. When leaders choose wholeness, they strengthen credibility now and secure a legacy later.

As we turn to the next chapter, remember: wholeness is the anchor. It grounds vision in integrity and strategy in trust. Without it, nothing endures; with it, everything becomes possible. Clarity of self creates clarity of sight—now let's name a future worth building together.

2 VISIONARY LEADERSHIP AND INNOVATION

Leaders are remembered not only for how they managed the present but for how they imagined the future. Visionary leadership lifts eyes beyond the immediate, while innovation creates the path to make vision real. Together, they shape the kind of futures that endure as legacy.

Earlier, we explored strategic vision as the anchor of leadership — the discipline of aligning choices with long-term purpose. Here, we turn to visionary leadership, which goes beyond alignment to imagination. Visionary leadership asks not only how we stay true to our mission, but how we create what does not yet exist. It is vision expanded into innovation. To see how vision actually moves people, start with a picture they can feel.

Casting a Future Worth Building

The room was quiet as I stood before a group who had grown weary of the day-to-day grind. We were meeting to discuss goals, but I could sense their focus was stuck on the immediate obstacles: deadlines, logistics, competing priorities. I knew that if I only talked about tasks, they would leave the same way they entered — tired and uninspired.

So I changed course. Instead of reviewing the checklist, I painted a picture: *"Imagine three years from now. Picture the kind of organization we can become if we commit ourselves to growth and innovation now. Imagine leaders stepping into roles we helped prepare them for. Imagine teams thriving because of the systems we set in place today. That's the future I see — and that's the future I believe we can build together."*

As I spoke, I watched heads lift. The atmosphere shifted from fatigue to possibility. People began nodding, leaning forward, exchanging glances that said, *"This matters."* What happened in that moment wasn't just motivation; it was vision. When leaders cast a compelling future, they create momentum that no checklist could ever achieve. That shift—from tasks to possibility—is the essence of visionary leadership.

The Nature of Visionary Leadership

Visionary leadership is the ability to see beyond immediate realities and articulate a future that inspires people to act. It is not simply about managing what *is* but about imagining what *could be*. Visionary leaders are not only strategists; they are storytellers. They give people a picture of the future that stirs hope, clarifies purpose, and makes sacrifice worthwhile. Imagination has to be anchored, or it drifts—anchored not in prediction, but in purpose.

Vision as Imagination Anchored in Purpose

Vision is not prediction—it is conviction. Forecasting attempts to anticipate what will happen; vision dares to name what *should* happen. It is less about reading trends and more about shaping possibilities. Visionary leaders ground their imagination in values, aligning the future they describe with the mission and identity of their people. This makes vision not a passing idea but a preferred future that people can believe in and commit to building together. Because purpose lives at every level, so must vision.

Vision at Every Level

Visionary leadership is not reserved for world leaders or CEOs. Any leader, in any context, can practice vision by aligning present actions with a meaningful future.

- A **supervisor** inspires vision by helping their team see how their daily work contributes to long-term impact.
- A **manager** inspires vision by naming a better way of serving clients, then mobilizing the team to reimagine processes.
- An **executive** inspires vision by painting a future for the entire organization that compels people to innovate and endure through change.

What matters most is not the scale of the vision but the clarity and conviction with which it is communicated. When people can see themselves in the future, effort turns into ownership.

Why Visionary Leadership Matters

Vision lifts people from fatigue to possibility. It transforms routine into a mission. It invites people to imagine a role in building something that does not yet exist but could—if they act with courage and creativity.

Holistic leaders understand this truth: vision is not optional for legacy. Leaders who focus only on immediate tasks may achieve results, but those who dare to imagine a better future create movements that endure. Vision is the seed of legacy—planted today, cultivated with conviction, and harvested in the generations to come. To make vision travel from words to work, lead by a few non-negotiable principles.

Principles of Visionary Leadership

Visionary leadership is not about lofty words or abstract dreams. It is about painting a picture of the future that people can see, believe, and commit themselves to build. For a vision to move beyond rhetoric, it must embody five principles: clarity, purpose, credibility, inspiration, and adaptability. When leaders live out these principles, they ignite a movement that outlasts tasks and transforms culture.

1. Clarity – Making the Future Visible

A vision must be clear enough that people can imagine themselves in it. Ambiguity breeds confusion, but clarity builds conviction. Clear vision answers practical questions: *Where are we going? What will it look like when we get there? What role do I play in making it real?*

- *Example:* A supervisor tells their team, "In the next year, I want us to become the department people come to for innovative solutions. That means each of us will identify one process we can improve, and we'll share progress monthly." Clear vision turns abstraction into action.

2. Purpose – Anchoring in Meaning, Not Just Metrics

Vision cannot be reduced to numbers or targets; it must connect to something more profound. Metrics track progress, but purpose inspires perseverance. Vision rooted in meaning helps people see that their work matters beyond immediate results.

- *Example:* A manager frames a sales goal not as "hitting numbers," but as "expanding access to products that genuinely improve our customers' lives." Purpose transforms tasks into a mission.

3. Credibility – Aligning Vision with Values and Actions

A vision is only as strong as the trust behind it. Leaders must embody the values they proclaim and align daily actions with long-term vision. If people see a gap between words and behavior, the vision collapses. Credibility gives vision weight.

- *Example:* An executive who casts a vision for sustainability but personally resists eco-friendly practices undermines credibility. By contrast, one who leads with consistent choices—reducing waste, investing in green solutions—builds trust in the vision.

4. Inspiration – Stirring Hope and Imagination

Vision must do more than inform; it must inspire. Facts engage the mind, but vision must also touch the heart. Inspirational vision lifts eyes from obstacles to possibilities and awakens imagination in those who may have stopped dreaming.

- *Example:* A nonprofit leader inspires volunteers by saying, "Every family we serve is one step closer to a safer home because of your efforts. Imagine a city where no child has to sleep in fear—that's the future we're building together."

5. Adaptability – Strong in Direction, Flexible in Execution

A strong vision provides direction, but flexibility ensures it survives changing circumstances. The destination may remain steady, but the path to get there may shift as conditions evolve. Leaders who cling rigidly to methods risk losing momentum; those who adapt keep vision alive.

- *Example:* A company's vision may be to become the most trusted provider in its industry. Economic shifts or new technology might change *how* they achieve it, but the vision remains intact because direction, not method, is the anchor.

When these five operate together, vision becomes a movement.

The Impact of Visionary Principles

When leaders embody clarity, purpose, credibility, inspiration, and adaptability, they create movements rather than just managing activity. Teams rally not because they are told to but because they believe in where they are going and who they are becoming.

Holistic leaders understand this: visionary leadership is not about grand speeches but about principles lived daily. When vision is clear, purposeful, credible, inspiring, and adaptable, it ignites not only progress but also legacy. And movements last only when aspiration meets execution.

Balancing Vision with Reality

Visionary leadership requires bold imagination, but vision without grounding can quickly lose credibility. People will follow a dream only if they believe it can be pursued in real life. Leaders who promise too much or paint a picture that feels impossible risk leaving their teams inspired in the moment but disillusioned in the long run.

Balancing vision with reality does not mean shrinking ambition—it means pairing aspiration with credibility. Vision must lift people's eyes beyond the present while also giving them a clear sense of how today's actions connect to tomorrow's outcomes. The best visions are both daring and believable.

Why Balance Matters

- **Overpromising leads to disappointment.** Teams lose trust when vision feels like empty rhetoric.
- **Underselling diminishes inspiration.** Playing it too safe robs people of the energy that comes from pursuing something greater than themselves.
- **Balance sustains momentum.** A bold vision paired with practical steps keeps hope alive while progress builds.

Practical Ways to Balance Vision and Reality
Here's how to hold boldness and believability together.

1. **Break Big Dreams into Small Wins.** Leaders articulate bold futures but also identify the first tangible steps forward. Small wins create momentum that makes the larger vision believable.
2. **Ground Vision in Values.** By tying vision to shared values, leaders ensure it feels authentic and aligned with purpose. Values keep vision from drifting into empty ambition.
3. **Test Feasibility.** Boldness must be paired with honest evaluation. Leaders ask, *"Do we have the resources, relationships, and resilience to take the next step?"*
4. **Communicate with Transparency.** It is better to say, *"This will be difficult, but here's how we will start,"* than to overpromise and underdeliver.

For Leaders at All Levels:
- A **supervisor** balances vision by helping their team see how daily tasks connect to long-term goals.
- A **manager** balances vision by setting quarterly targets that align with the larger organizational dream.
- An **executive** balances vision by casting bold futures while providing realistic roadmaps that show how the vision will be achieved.

Holistic leaders understand that vision without realism becomes fantasy, and realism without vision becomes routine. The legacy of visionary leadership comes not from choosing one or the other but from holding both together—dreaming boldly while guiding people step by step into a future they can believe in and help build. Balance sets the posture; frameworks give you handles.

Frameworks for Vision and Innovation
These frameworks offer leaders practical ways to translate vision into action. Each provides a different lens for imagining the future and moving from ideas to implementation. By combining creativity with structure, they help leaders not only dream but also design pathways that bring those dreams to life.

Design Thinking: Design Thinking moves innovation from theory into practice through a structured yet flexible process: *Empathize, Define, Ideate, Prototype, and Test.* I use Design Thinking as a people-first way to create change. We start with empathy, listening until we can state someone's need better than they can. We name the real problem, not just its symptoms. We brainstorm boldly, then test small with rough drafts that invite feedback. Finally, we learn fast, keeping what works and discarding what doesn't.

Futures Thinking: Futures Thinking is the discipline of exploring multiple scenarios to prepare for uncertainty. Instead of predicting a single outcome, leaders imagine a range of plausible futures—economic shifts, technological advances, cultural changes—and consider how their organization might adapt in each.

For example, a leader might ask: *"What if automation replaces half our current roles? What if customer expectations shift radically? What if climate policy reshapes our supply chain?"* By rehearsing these scenarios in advance, leaders reduce surprise and increase agility.

Futures Thinking does not eliminate uncertainty, but it equips leaders to face it with confidence. It broadens vision, stretches imagination, and prevents complacency. Leaders who practice this discipline leave a legacy of organizations that are resilient not because they avoided change, but because they prepared for it.

Blue Ocean Strategy: Blue Ocean Strategy challenges leaders to stop competing in crowded, "red oceans" where rivals fight over shrinking margins. Instead, it invites them to create "blue oceans"—entirely new spaces of opportunity where competition is irrelevant.

Classic examples include Cirque du Soleil, which reinvented circus entertainment by combining theater, dance, and acrobatics for adult audiences, or Apple's iTunes, which transformed music distribution. In each case, the leaders asked: *"What can we eliminate? What can we reduce? What can we raise? What can we create?"*

For holistic leaders, Blue Ocean Strategy is not only about capturing markets but also about serving people in new and imaginative ways. It fosters courage, vision, and creativity. Leaders who embrace it leave behind more than incremental improvements—they leave industries and communities transformed by new possibilities.

Vision Statements: A vision statement is more than corporate language; it is a concise picture of the future that inspires and guides. Unlike mission statements, which define purpose in the present, vision statements paint what the future will look like if the mission is lived out faithfully.

An effective vision statement is clear, memorable, and compelling. For example: *"By 2030, every child in our city will have access to safe housing and quality education."* Such a statement not only directs strategy but also galvanizes commitment by connecting daily work to something larger than immediate tasks.

Leaders who craft and communicate strong vision statements ensure their teams are not simply executing tasks but building toward a future worth striving for. Over time, these statements become rallying cries that outlive the leader, anchoring the organization in its enduring purpose.

Innovation Cycles: Innovation is not a one-time breakthrough but a disciplined cycle: trial, reflection, refinement, and scaling. Leaders encourage their teams to try new ideas in small ways, reflect honestly on results, refine based on lessons learned, and scale what works.

This rhythm normalizes learning and reduces fear of failure. It tells teams: *"Experimentation is not risky—it is expected."* Leaders who champion innovation cycles avoid the extremes of endless brainstorming with no results or rigid planning that stifles creativity. Instead, they create steady streams of progress, where ideas are continuously tested, improved, and expanded.

Over time, innovation cycles become cultural DNA. They ensure that the organization is never static but constantly evolving. Leaders who establish this rhythm leave a legacy of teams that don't just adapt to change but drive it. These lenses make vision practical; now, here's why innovation must become a habit.

The Innovation Imperative

Vision without innovation quickly becomes irrelevant. Innovation is the practice of turning vision into reality by creating new solutions, systems, or approaches. It is not change for its own sake, but purposeful creativity aligned with mission and values.

I've seen teams struggle because they clung to familiar patterns even as circumstances shifted. What once worked no longer did, but the reluctance to innovate held them back. By contrast, when I encouraged a group to reimagine their processes, the energy returned. They discovered not only better methods but also renewed ownership of the work.

Innovation requires courage because it asks people to step into the unknown. But it also requires discipline, because not every new idea is strategic. Visionary leaders create cultures where innovation is encouraged, tested, and refined until it serves the greater purpose.

Frameworks alone, however, do not create visionary leaders. They are tools—but tools require courage, creativity, and consistency to be effective. What makes vision and innovation powerful is not simply knowing the models but practicing them daily, inviting others into the process, and grounding them in values. When leaders take these frameworks off the page and weave them into real conversations, decisions, and strategies, vision stops being an abstract idea and becomes a lived experience that shapes culture and legacy. Culture changes when innovation is demystified and practiced daily.

Innovation as Everyday Practice

When people hear the word *innovation*, they often think of breakthrough technologies, billion-dollar startups, or industry-shifting inventions. But in reality, innovation is not confined to research labs or executive suites. It is a daily practice available to every leader and every team. Innovation happens whenever people ask, *"How can we do this better?"* and are given the freedom to explore answers.

The Myth of Innovation as Extraordinary

Too often, leaders dismiss innovation because it feels out of reach. They assume it requires specialized teams, advanced tools, or massive resources. The truth is that most enduring innovations begin small— new ways of holding meetings, new methods for solving customer problems, new approaches to collaboration. Over time, these small shifts compound into cultural change.

Innovation in Everyday Leadership
- A **supervisor** encourages a team to rethink the way shifts are scheduled, making it more equitable and efficient.
- A **manager** experiments with a new way of running performance reviews, focusing on coaching instead of compliance.
- An **executive** invites frontline employees to pitch ideas for improving customer service, and then pilots one of those ideas.

Each of these examples demonstrates that innovation is not reserved for dramatic breakthroughs—it is embedded in daily leadership. If you want everyday innovation, create everyday invitations.

Practical Ways to Foster Everyday Innovation
1. **Ask Better Questions.** Instead of asking, *"What's wrong?"* ask, *"What's possible?"* Shifting questions sparks creative thinking.
2. **Reward Curiosity.** Celebrate not only successful outcomes but also bold attempts. When people see that risk-taking is valued, creativity multiplies.
3. **Start Small.** Encourage low-cost, low-risk experiments. A simple pilot project can build momentum and confidence.
4. **Create Space.** Innovation rarely happens when schedules are packed to the brim. Leaders must intentionally carve out time for exploration and reflection.
5. **Share Stories.** Highlight examples of everyday innovation across the organization so that people see creativity as part of the culture.

With the culture ready, use a few structured tools—without repeating what you've already learned.

Why Everyday Innovation Matters
- It democratizes creativity—everyone can contribute, not just a few specialists.
- It builds adaptability by normalizing experimentation.
- It prevents stagnation, ensuring teams continuously evolve rather than waiting for a crisis to force change.

Holistic leaders understand that innovation is not a rare event but a rhythm. It is not about dramatic reinvention once a decade but about steady, consistent improvement that keeps teams vibrant and futures open. By practicing innovation daily, leaders create cultures where creativity becomes second nature and legacy grows not from one breakthrough but from a thousand small improvements that endure. Frameworks give structure; personal disciplines keep them alive.

Personal Practices for Visionary Leaders
- **Practice Imagination:** Regularly set aside time to think beyond current realities.
- **Stay Rooted in Purpose:** Anchor every vision in mission and values.
- **Communicate Relentlessly:** Share vision consistently until it becomes culture.
- **Model Curiosity:** Ask questions that spark creativity and invite exploration.
- **Balance Boldness with Practicality:** Pair big ideas with actionable steps.

These habits change rooms, not just plans.

Vision and Innovation in Practice
I recall leading a brainstorming session where the energy was low at first. People were hesitant to speak, fearing their ideas might be dismissed. I intentionally created space by saying, *"Right now, there are no bad ideas. Let's fill the board with possibilities, no matter how unrealistic they may sound."*

Within minutes, the atmosphere shifted. Ideas flowed. Laughter emerged. Out of that free space, a genuinely innovative solution surfaced — one that became a turning point for the project. The key wasn't that I had the answer; it was that I created an environment where vision and creativity could flourish. What begins as a moment of imagination becomes the memory a culture repeats—that's legacy.

Vision, Innovation, and Legacy

A leader's legacy is not measured solely by the goals they achieved in their tenure but by the future they enabled. Holistic leaders should ask the following: *Did I create conditions where others could imagine more, risk more, and achieve more? Did I leave behind a culture of creativity and courage that continued long after you stepped away?* Legacy is not only about outcomes—it is about the possibilities leaders set in motion.

Why Vision and Innovation Together Shape Legacy
- **Vision sustains focus.** It keeps people anchored in meaning.
- **Innovation fuels progress.** It turns imagination into tangible results.
- **Together, they multiply influence.** They ensure that leadership is not a temporary role but a force that carries forward.

For Leaders at All Levels:
- A **supervisor** leaves a legacy when they teach their team to see beyond the checklist and imagine better ways of working.
- A **manager** leaves a legacy when they create space for employees to pilot new ideas that improve both culture and outcomes.
- An **executive** leaves a legacy when they establish systems where innovation becomes part of organizational DNA rather than a passing project.

When leaders combine vision and innovation with integrity, they build futures that endure. They leave behind not only strategies but also a spirit—a way of thinking, imagining, and creating—that continues shaping generations. The most powerful legacy a leader can leave is not merely a completed project or a finished plan, but a culture that keeps dreaming boldly and innovating faithfully long after the leader is gone.

Holistic leaders understand this truth: vision and innovation are not about personal achievement but about multiplication. They ask not only *"What did I accomplish?"* but *"What possibilities did I unleash for others?"* That is the mark of a leader whose influence transcends time and continues to inspire future generations.

From Theory to Practice

Visionary leadership cannot remain in the realm of imagination. A compelling picture of the future loses power if it is not paired with courageous action. Vision without practice remains an idea; innovation without discipline becomes noise. To turn vision into reality, leaders must translate imagination into daily habits and organizational rhythms that make creativity sustainable and meaningful.

Five Practices for Visionary Innovators

1. **Cast Vision Boldly**

    Vision must be spoken with clarity and conviction. Leaders cannot assume people know where the organization is going—they must hear it repeatedly and consistently. Bold casting means painting a picture large enough to inspire, yet clear enough for people to imagine themselves in it.

    - *Example:* A supervisor says, "By the end of the year, our team will be known as the group that solved this persistent problem." A manager shares, "Within three years, our department will redefine how we serve customers." Bold vision clarifies direction and sparks commitment.

2. **Foster Creativity**

    Creativity flourishes only in environments where people feel safe to share ideas without fear of ridicule or dismissal. Visionary leaders create those environments by inviting input, encouraging brainstorming, and recognizing effort, not just outcomes.

    - *Example:* A manager holds a monthly "innovation hour" where anyone can propose an idea, no matter how rough. An executive rewards teams not just for successful projects but also for courageous attempts, signaling that innovation is part of culture, not a gamble.

3. **Test and Refine**
   Visionary leaders know that most ideas arrive unfinished. Instead of waiting for perfection, they move quickly from concept to prototype, learning through trial, error, and feedback. This cycle of experimentation makes innovation less intimidating and more practical.
   - *Example:* A leader pilots a new process with one team before scaling it across the organization. Early refinements reduce risk and increase buy-in, making the vision tangible step by step.
4. **Stay Anchored**
   Not every new idea is worth pursuing. Visionary leadership requires discipline to filter innovation through mission and values. Staying anchored prevents distraction, ensuring that creativity serves purpose rather than novelty.
   - *Example:* An executive evaluates a promising opportunity by asking, *"Does this align with who we are and the future we want to create?"* When innovation stays tethered to identity, it strengthens culture rather than diluting it.
5. **Connect to Legacy**
   Visionary leadership always looks beyond the present. Leaders frame vision and innovation as investments in the future—not just quick wins but seeds planted for the next generation. Connecting vision to legacy gives meaning to risk and endurance to effort.
   - *Example:* A nonprofit leader tells their team, *"The systems we're building now will outlast us. Future families will benefit because we dared to think differently today."*

Do them consistently, and vision stops being an event—it becomes culture.

Why These Practices Matter

Visionary leadership is not measured by the brilliance of an idea but by the persistence of habits that bring ideas to life. Leaders who cast boldly, foster creativity, test and refine, stay anchored, and connect to legacy move beyond talk. They create momentum, shape culture, and ensure that vision and innovation leave a lasting imprint.

Holistic leaders understand this: visionary leadership is not about occasional bursts of inspiration but about disciplined practices that make the future real. When imagination and action meet, legacies are written. Watch for the common failure modes that quietly drain momentum.

Pitfalls and Best Practices
Pitfall 1: Chasing Novelty
- Example: Implementing every new idea without a strategy.
- Best Practice: Filter innovation through vision and values.

Pitfall 2: Overpromising in Vision
- Example: Painting an unrealistic picture that creates disappointment.
- Best Practice: Cast bold visions that are inspiring yet credible.

Pitfall 3: Ignoring Execution
- Example: Talking about innovation without building systems to deliver it.
- Best Practice: Balance vision with disciplined follow-through.

Pitfall 4: Stifling Creativity
- Example: Dismissing new ideas too quickly.
- Best Practice: Encourage brainstorming before evaluation.

Clarify your next move with a few focused questions.

Reflective Questions
1. How clearly can you articulate the future you are working toward?
2. Do you create safe spaces for innovation, or do people fear sharing bold ideas?
3. What practices help you balance vision with execution?
4. How do you filter innovation through mission and values?
5. What kind of legacy will your vision and innovation leave behind?

Journaling Prompts
- Write about a time you cast a vision that inspired others.
- Reflect on one innovation your team implemented. What made it successful?
- Journal about your own resistance to change. How can you overcome it?
- Describe the future legacy you want your leadership to create.

90-Day Visionary Leadership Plan

Month 1 – Cast Vision
- Write or refine your personal leadership vision statement.
- Share it with your team and invite feedback.

Month 2 – Spark Innovation
- Facilitate one design thinking session.
- Encourage bold ideas by setting aside time for brainstorming.

Month 3 – Anchor and Act
- Choose one innovative idea to prototype.
- Communicate how it connects to your mission and values.
- Celebrate progress and share stories of innovation.

Ninety days of small, steady practice creates belief—and belief sustains bold vision. By the end of 90 days, you will not only have sharpened your ability to cast vision but also cultivated a culture of innovation that ensures your leadership leaves an enduring legacy.

This practice grows results now and reputation later—the shape of how you'll be remembered. Vision without innovation fades, and innovation without vision drifts. But together, they shape futures worth building. Leaders who practice both are remembered not for managing what was but for creating what could be — and that is the essence of legacy. Vision answers why and where; strategy answers how and when. The next chapter turns aspiration into alignment.

3 STRATEGIC THINKING FOR LEGACY-MINDED LEADERS

Every enduring act of leadership begins with vision. Without vision, leaders react to the demands of the moment; with vision, they create futures that inspire others to believe and to build. Vision is the foundation of legacy. In this chapter, we focus on strategic vision—the ability to anchor daily decisions in mission, values, and long-term purpose. Strategic vision provides clarity and alignment for the present while shaping a future that outlasts the leader.

Leadership, at its essence, is not about personality or charisma. It is about clarity and courage. It is the discipline of seeing further than others can see, articulating what is possible, and aligning today's actions to tomorrow's outcomes. Strategic thinking transforms leadership from the mere management of tasks into the building of a legacy that can endure beyond the leader's tenure.

Strategic vision provides direction. It draws together scattered efforts, prevents the drift of distraction, and rallies people around what matters most. Vision without strategy can remain a dream, never translated into action. Strategy without vision becomes lifeless management, checking boxes without meaning. Legacy-minded leaders hold vision and strategy in balance, weaving them into a cycle of inspiration and execution. Before tools and templates, the first question is simpler: why does strategy matter at every level?

Why Strategic Leadership Matters

Why does strategic leadership matter? Because without it, even well-intentioned leaders find themselves consumed by urgency instead of guided by purpose. They end up solving today's problems while neglecting tomorrow's possibilities. They may keep the lights on, but they fail to ignite lasting impact.

Strategic leadership matters for executives and entrepreneurs, yes—but also for frontline supervisors and new managers. The decisions made by those closest to the ground ripple outward, shaping culture, efficiency, and trust. A new supervisor deciding how to hold her first team meeting is practicing strategic leadership if she anchors that meeting in clarity of purpose, values, and goals. A mid-level manager choosing how to allocate resources across departments is either reinforcing or undermining the long-term vision. An entrepreneur writing the business plan is laying down the framework that will either build a legacy or collapse under short-term thinking.

Strategic leadership prevents drift. It forces leaders to ask not only, *What do we need to do now?* but also, *How does this decision align with who we are, what we value, and where we are going?* Without that discipline, leaders operate in what Chris Argyris called "single-loop learning"—fixing surface-level problems without questioning underlying assumptions. Strategic leadership pushes us into "double-loop learning"—asking not just *how* to fix the problem, but *why* the problem exists, *what assumptions underlie our current system*, and *how we can redesign our approach to create lasting change.*

Legacy is not built by accident. It is built by leaders who anticipate, align, and prepare—not merely react. Strategic leadership is not simply about planning or managing. It is about **casting vision**—seeing a future that does not yet exist, mobilizing people to believe in it, and aligning resources to bring it to life. It requires a leader who can hold the tension of today's challenges and tomorrow's opportunities, and who can navigate complexity without losing sight of values. With the case made, we can set a strategy in its relational context: leaders and followers together.

As the foundation of holistic leadership, strategic thinking ensures that decisions are made with clarity, rooted in ethics, and driven by both long-term goals and immediate realities.

Strategic leadership is not a solo pursuit. It is a relationship between leaders and followers, between organizations and communities, between vision and execution. To understand this relationship, we must first explore how leadership and followership have evolved and why their interdependence matters for leaders who desire to leave a legacy.

The Evolution of Leadership and Followership

To appreciate strategic leadership, it is crucial to understand how leadership and followership have evolved. For much of human history, leadership was equated with authority and domination. Kings ruled by decree, generals commanded by rank, and followers obeyed out of duty or fear. The early twentieth century carried these assumptions into organizations, where leadership was often reduced to a matter of position.

By the mid-twentieth century, scholars sought to define leadership by traits: intelligence, charisma, and decisiveness. Leaders were assumed to be born, not made. Over time, research shifted toward behavior, identifying what leaders actually do rather than who they are. In the 1970s, James MacGregor Burns advanced a transformational model of leadership—describing it as a reciprocal, moral process of mobilizing people around purpose and values. Transformational leaders elevated followers to pursue more than self-interest; they inspired them to pursue the greater good.

Equally important has been the reframing of followership. For decades, followers were seen as passive participants, supporting actors to the leader's starring role. But work by Robert Kelley and Ira Chaleff challenged this view, showing that effective followership is active, engaged, and courageous. Followers choose whether to align with a vision, whether to challenge assumptions, and whether to contribute their energy toward shared goals.

Leadership and followership are not opposites; they are interdependent roles in a dynamic system. Legacy-minded leaders understand this. They cultivate environments where followers are empowered to think, speak, and grow. In doing so, they multiply leadership capacity across the organization.

This evolution teaches us that leadership divorced from followership is meaningless. Leaders cannot exist without followers, and followers shape the legitimacy of leaders. Visionary leadership is only as strong as the collective belief and participation it inspires. Context frames the work; definition focuses it. Here's what strategic leadership is—practically.

The Nature of Strategic Leadership

Strategic leadership isn't a title—it's the discipline of aligning purpose with practice across people and systems. Strategic leadership is the discipline of aligning mission, vision, values, and goals with both internal strengths and external realities. It requires what scholars call a **dual lens**: managing present operations while also anticipating future trends and positioning the organization for long-term success. Strategic leaders understand that their decisions have ripple effects — not just within the organization but across industries, communities, and even global contexts.

Strategic leaders:
- **Cast Vision** – Articulate a compelling, future-oriented direction.
- **Align Mission** – Ensure everyday actions reflect the organization's purpose.
- **Make Ethical Decisions** – Weigh choices with moral clarity.
- **Develop Systemic Awareness** – Understand how internal and external systems interact.

When vision becomes a system, culture starts to carry strategy between meetings. Leaders who master strategic leadership do not see vision as a slogan but as a system. They weave it into meetings, performance reviews, and hallway conversations until it becomes part of the culture. Strategic thinking, when practiced consistently, transforms organizations from the inside out. This leadership does not occur by accident. It is intentional, reflective, and deeply attuned to the people it serves. Strategic leaders don't just forecast the future—they help create it.

Strategic Thinking as a Way of Seeing

If strategic leadership is the discipline, strategic thinking is the lens. It changes how leaders notice patterns, test assumptions, and connect today's choices to tomorrow's legacy. Strategic thinking is not an occasional exercise for a retreat; it is a way of seeing. It is the ability to look at daily decisions through the lens of long-term purpose. Strategic leaders hold the tension of the immediate and the eventual. They respond to today's demands without losing sight of tomorrow's legacy.

A strategic thinker consistently asks:
- What forces are shaping our environment?
- Which assumptions underlie our current approach?
- What opportunities and risks are emerging that we have not considered?
- How do today's actions build or erode tomorrow's legacy?

Strategic thinking blends analysis and imagination. It is disciplined enough to weigh evidence and anticipate consequences, but imaginative enough to challenge assumptions and envision new futures. It draws on data and discernment, logic and creativity.

This combination distinguishes managers from legacy leaders. Managers solve problems. Legacy leaders create possibilities. Possibility still needs guardrails—values give strategy its spine.

The Intersection of Strategy and Values

Clarity without character can still go astray. The next move is to connect strategy to values so direction and integrity reinforce each other. One of the greatest temptations for leaders is expediency—choosing short-term gain over long-term integrity. However, truly transformational leaders operate from a firm value system. They understand that a strategy devoid of ethics leads to hollow victories and short-lived gains. In contrast, when values and strategy are intertwined, the result is authentic leadership that inspires trust and long-term commitment.

Strategic leaders ask:
- Does this align with our organizational values?
- Who will be impacted by this decision?
- What are the ethical implications?
- How do we ensure equity and inclusiveness in implementation?

These questions are not meant to slow leaders down but to sharpen them. When decisions are filtered through values, they gain credibility. People may not always agree with the path chosen, but they will trust a leader who demonstrates consistency between words and actions. Strategic leaders understand that their decisions signal more than priorities—they signal culture. These questions anchor the leader in a moral framework that transcends personal ambition and prioritizes collective well-being.

I once supported a workgroup wrestling with a decision that could have made us look more efficient on paper, but would have required cutting corners on compliance. On the surface, it seemed like a quick win. But I knew if we compromised our values here, it would set a precedent we couldn't come back from. I told the team, *"We cannot sacrifice integrity for convenience. If this doesn't align with our values, it's not the right move — no matter how good it looks in the short run."* In that moment, I saw relief on their faces. People want leaders who anchor decisions in values because it gives them permission to act with integrity themselves.

These questions only have power if they become a daily practice. That's why we anchor strategy in values—not as slogans, but as operational commitments. The next move is to make values visible and trackable in daily leadership.

Anchoring Strategy in Values

Values are the compass of strategic leadership. Without values, strategy devolves into opportunism. History is filled with organizations that compromised on ethics for short-term wins, only to forfeit trust and longevity.

Values define what matters most. They answer the question: *What will we refuse to compromise, even under pressure?* When uncertainty rises, values stabilize. They allow leaders to say, *We may not control every outcome, but we know who we are and what we stand for.*

Operationalizing values requires more than stating them. Leaders must translate values into behaviors, decisions, and rituals. This is where practical tools become essential.

Tool Deep Dive: The Integrity Ledger™

To make values visible, leaders need simple, repeatable tools. The Integrity Ledger™ turns promises into measurable practice, and is a simple but powerful discipline: leaders record every promise made—to their team, stakeholders, or themselves—and track whether it was kept. On the surface, it looks like a logbook. In practice, it becomes a mirror of accountability and a living record of trust.

Far too often, leaders underestimate how much weight their words carry. What may seem like a passing comment—"I'll get back to you on that," or "I'll look into it"—lands as a promise in the mind of a follower. When it goes unfulfilled, even unintentionally, it erodes trust grain by grain. Over time, those grains pile up into a mountain of skepticism. The Integrity Ledger™ prevents that drift. It forces leaders to recognize that words matter, that promises are contracts, and that credibility is built or broken one commitment at a time.

How to Use the Integrity Ledger™

1. **At the start of each week, write down all commitments made.**
   These can be large or small—approving a budget, following up with a client, or scheduling a check-in with a team member. Nothing is too minor if someone is depending on it.
2. **At week's end, review which promises were kept and which were missed.**
   This review creates clarity. It reveals where intentions matched actions and where gaps emerged. Even one missed commitment can highlight a pattern that needs attention.
3. **Share results openly, inviting feedback from the team.**
   Transparency is what makes the Integrity Ledger™ powerful. When leaders share their ledger—successes and failures—they send a message: "I am accountable to you as much as you are to me." This vulnerability strengthens psychological safety.

4. **Notice patterns—are you overpromising? Are certain areas consistently neglected?**
   The ledger quickly reveals blind spots. Maybe you consistently deliver on project-related commitments but often fail to follow up on people-related ones. Or perhaps your ambition leads you to say yes too quickly, stretching your credibility thin.
5. **Adjust practices to ensure commitments are realistic and values-driven.**
   The point is not perfection but alignment. By noticing and adjusting, leaders ensure that promises reflect both capacity and values.

Why It Works

This simple act builds credibility. Over time, teams learn that leadership promises are trustworthy. The ledger becomes a mirror for accountability. It makes integrity visible, not abstract.

Imagine walking into a meeting and being able to say, "Here are the commitments I made this week, and here's how I did." The team not only hears about integrity; they see it in practice. Over time, this discipline changes culture. People begin holding themselves accountable in the same way. Trust multiplies, performance improves, and alignment strengthens.

A Personal Example

I once led a project where deadlines were tight and expectations high. Team members had voiced frustration that previous leaders promised resources that never materialized. I began keeping an Integrity Ledger™—not only for myself but also as a shared document. At each weekly check-in, I reviewed what I had promised and reported progress. Some weeks, I had to admit, "I missed this one, and here's how I'll correct it."

At first, the team was cautious. They had heard promises before. But as weeks turned into months, something shifted. Team members began saying, "I'll add that to my ledger too." What started as my personal discipline became a team-wide culture of accountability. We not only met the project goals but also rebuilt trust that had been eroded over the years.

Leadership at Every Level

The Integrity Ledger™ is not just for executives. A new supervisor can use it to track promises to her first team. A mid-level manager can use it to balance competing stakeholder demands. An entrepreneur can use it to stay grounded in the chaos of building something new. At every level, the Ledger cultivates wholeness by aligning words and actions. Integrity grounds the leader; conditions test that ground. Enter VUCA.

Integrity grounds us internally; context challenges us externally. The environment we lead in is volatile, uncertain, complex, and ambiguous—and strategy must account for that reality.

Strategic Leadership in a VUCA World

Today's leaders operate in a **VUCA world**: volatile, uncertain, complex, and ambiguous. This environment demands leaders who can anchor decisions in values while navigating shifting circumstances.

- **Volatility** requires agility. Leaders must adjust quickly when conditions change.
- **Uncertainty** requires adaptability. Leaders must move forward even without complete clarity.
- **Complexity** requires systems thinking. Leaders must consider interdependent parts and long-term consequences.
- **Ambiguity** requires discernment. Leaders must act when cause and effect are unclear.

Strategic leaders navigate VUCA by scanning broadly, interpreting patterns, and aligning decisions with mission. They focus on a few must-win priorities instead of scattering energy. They communicate clearly and consistently to reduce confusion and anxiety.

The Holistic Leadership Cycle™

Surviving VUCA requires more than heroic effort. It requires a leadership engine that multiplies capacity over time. The Holistic Leadership Cycle™ illustrates how legacy is multiplied. Leaders develop followers into leaders who, in turn, develop others, creating a continuous cycle of growth. Strategic thinking is the entry point.

When leaders model clarity of purpose and values-based decision-making, followers learn to think strategically themselves. Over time, those followers step into leadership roles, carrying forward the same practices. In this way, leadership becomes embedded in culture, not dependent on a single personality.

In my own leadership journey, I saw this cycle firsthand. By investing time in developing one promising team member—sharing strategy, values, and decision-making frameworks—I saw that individual later mentor others. The culture began to shift. Strategic thinking spread through the team not by decree but by example. One investment created ripples of leadership capacity. The cycle proves itself under pressure—that's where strategy becomes transformational.

Transformational Strategy in Action

Strategic leadership is most visible when theory meets crisis. When I worked with a cross-functional group facing uncertainty in a major initiative, I saw firsthand how strategy must address operational realities while also engaging broader questions of equity, access, and long-term resilience. A holistic leader anticipates needs before they arise, communicates transparently, and empowers teams to act decisively within a shared framework of values.

In practice, transformational strategy involves:
- **Environmental Scanning:** Identifying external trends and their potential impact.
- **Organizational Assessment:** Evaluating internal capabilities and vulnerabilities.
- **Scenario Planning:** Creating models for various futures and preparing for each.
- **Inclusive Engagement:** Involving diverse voices in strategic conversations.
- **Agility with Accountability:** Making room for adaptability without sacrificing integrity.

By embracing these practices, leaders become proactive architects of the future rather than reactive managers of the present. And none of it is sustainable without a moral steering wheel.

Ethics as a Strategic Imperative

Strategy without ethics may move fast, but it doesn't endure. Ethics is not a brake; it is the steering wheel. Ethical leadership is not an abstract ideal. It is a strategic necessity. Organizations led by ethical leaders report higher trust, lower risk, and increased engagement. Ethical decision-making should be embedded into every strategic framework, with leaders modeling transparency, accountability, and moral courage.

Three characteristics define manageable strategic risks:
- **Uncertainty:** Recognizing potential unknowns and preparing contingencies.
- **Loss:** Assessing the cost of inaction or missteps.
- **Time Component:** Establishing a clear window for action and reflection.

Ethics is not a pause in the process; it is the compass. Strategic leaders who understand these dimensions are better equipped to navigate volatility without compromising integrity.

Strategic Vision

With ethics steering, vision determines the route. A clear, compelling picture of the future turns scattered effort into focused momentum. Strategic vision is more than a statement — it is a picture of the future that guides decision-making and inspires action. Leaders who develop strategic vision provide clarity about where the organization is heading and why it matters.

I have often seen vision statements written and then forgotten in binders. The difference between a forgotten statement and a living vision is practice. Leaders must bring vision into the daily rhythms of decision-making and team conversations, so that it guides not just what is said but what is done.

Steps to Creating a Strategic Vision
1. **Clarify Core Purpose:** Begin with mission and values.
2. **Scan the Environment:** Assess internal strengths and external realities.
3. **Imagine the Future:** Ask, *"What do we want to be true five years from now?"*
4. **Engage Others:** Invite diverse perspectives to shape and refine the vision.
5. **Articulate Clearly:** State the vision in simple, compelling language.
6. **Align Action:** Ensure daily practices connect back to the vision.
7. **Revisit and Refine:** Adapt vision as contexts change while staying true to core values.

Example of a Strategic Vision
"Our organization will be recognized as the trusted partner that redefines housing solutions for working families. By 2030, we will expand into 10 new markets, not only increasing access to affordable, quality homes but also investing in community programs that strengthen education and financial literacy. Every initiative we undertake will align with our core values of integrity, service, and innovation. Success will not be measured solely by units managed or profits earned, but by the number of families whose futures are improved because of our leadership. This vision guides today's decisions while anchoring us in the legacy we are committed to leaving tomorrow."

A vision only lives if it has a beat.

Building Strategic Rhythm
Cadence turns intention into habit. Strategies often fail because they remain abstract. To succeed, strategy must become rhythm. Leaders embed strategy into weekly, monthly, and quarterly cadences.
- **Mission Monday:** Begin each week by reminding teams of purpose and the top three priorities.
- **Mid-Week Metrics:** Review dashboards, unblock decisions, and reset if needed.
- **Friday Learnings:** Reflect on successes and failures, update the decision log.

These rhythms create predictability, reduce anxiety, and keep strategy alive. Rhythm holds the plan; EQ holds the leader.

Emotional Intelligence and Strategic Clarity

Even the best rhythms fail if the leader is reactive. Emotional intelligence keeps strategy steady when pressure spikes. No framework can compensate for a leader who lacks emotional intelligence. Strategic clarity begins with emotional clarity. Leaders who cannot manage their own reactions undermine trust.

The **Pause–Name–Choose** technique helps:
1. **Pause** before reacting.
2. **Name** the emotion honestly.
3. **Choose** the response most aligned with values and strategy.

By modeling self-awareness, leaders show teams that strategy is not just intellectual—it is emotional and relational. With steadiness in place, choices can match values under pressure.

Strategic Decision-Making

Rhythms create stability; decisions create direction. Here's how to choose in ways that reflect both values and vision. Strategic decision-making is the discipline of choosing actions that align with vision and values while balancing short-term needs with long-term goals.

Filters for Strategic Decisions
- **Mission Test:** Does this align with our core purpose?
- **Values Test:** Does this reflect who we are?
- **Impact Test:** Who benefits and who bears the cost?
- **Legacy Test:** Will this choice matter ten years from now?

Models for Practice
- **SWOT Analysis:** Identify strengths, weaknesses, opportunities, threats.
- **Predictive Index and Personality Insights:** Understand team dynamics to make informed choices.
- **Scenario Planning:** Map out best-case, worst-case, and likely outcomes.

Strategic decision-making is where vision becomes real. Every decision is a test of whether leaders will choose what is easy or what is aligned. Legacy is not built by one grand vision but by thousands of small, consistent decisions that reinforce it. Strategic leaders make decisions not in isolation but with awareness of ripple effects, long-term implications, and cultural impact. Now let's turn the concepts into repeatable behaviors.

From Theory to Practice (Toolkit)
To help leaders at every level, the following tools translate strategy into repeatable behaviors—so alignment is visible and teachable. Strategic leadership must move from aspiration to action. This includes equipping leaders with the tools and skills to make informed decisions, foster alignment across teams, and measure success with both qualitative and quantitative metrics.

Leaders can practice it through tools such as:

Leadership Covenant – A covenant personalizes leadership: it clarifies what I promise and how I'll be held to it. A Leadership Covenant is not simply a policy document; it is a living promise. At its core, it represents a leader's explicit commitment to live and lead with integrity, transparency, and accountability. Unlike compliance manuals or handbooks, a covenant is deeply personal. It articulates what a leader believes and how those beliefs translate into daily decisions. For example, a covenant might read: *"I will tell the truth even when it costs me, listen to understand before speaking, and use my influence to build others rather than elevate myself."*

This clarity reduces ambiguity in decision-making and fosters trust even in moments of crisis. Leaders who return to their covenant regularly—re-reading it, sharing it with new team members, and holding themselves publicly accountable—create cultures where values are not abstract aspirations but tangible commitments. Over time, the covenant becomes a legacy document, reminding future leaders of the promises that shaped the organization's character.

SWOT Analysis – If covenant defines character, SWOT clarifies context—what we're good at, where we're vulnerable, and what's changing around us. A SWOT analysis—strengths, weaknesses, opportunities, and threats—has long been a staple in strategic planning. But when wielded by holistic leaders, it becomes more than a business exercise; it is a leadership discipline. SWOT forces leaders to step back and take a balanced, 360-degree view of their reality. It compels them to acknowledge what is working well, where vulnerabilities lie, where the future may open doors, and what risks could undermine progress.

For example, an organization might identify a strength as *"a loyal, purpose-driven workforce,"* while a weakness could be *"outdated digital infrastructure."* Opportunities might include *"emerging markets hungry for our solutions,"* and threats could be *"new competitors leveraging technology to deliver faster, cheaper alternatives."*

What makes SWOT powerful is not the chart itself but the conversations it sparks. Leaders who conduct a SWOT with transparency invite teams to own both the good and the difficult. They demonstrate that acknowledging weakness is not failure but foresight, and that recognizing threats is not pessimism but prudence. Done consistently, SWOT becomes a rhythm of resilience—an early warning system that guides leaders to adapt without losing their long-term vision.

Alignment Workshops – With context clear, alignment workshops turn insight into shared commitment. Alignment workshops are dedicated spaces where stakeholders pause the daily grind to recalibrate. These gatherings are not brainstorming sessions for new ideas; they are alignment sessions for existing priorities. The central question is: *"Are we truly moving in the same direction?"*

During a typical alignment workshop, leaders bring together cross-functional teams—executives, managers, and key contributors—to review the organization's vision and priorities. Through facilitated dialogue, they uncover misalignments, resolve competing agendas, and co-create a set of shared commitments. The result is not just a clearer plan but a stronger sense of collective ownership.

For instance, a workshop might conclude with three unified strategic priorities for the year, each linked to clear outcomes and supported by champions from different departments. But perhaps the most valuable outcome is relational: people leave the room knowing they were heard and that their contributions matter.

Alignment workshops remind leaders that unity is not automatic; it must be built intentionally. Leaders who host them regularly reinforce that clarity, collaboration, and shared ownership are non-negotiable. Over time, these workshops shift culture from silos and competition to synergy and collective achievement.

KPIs (Key Performance Indicators) – Commitment needs evidence. Key Performance Indicators tell us if our walk matches our talk. KPIs are often reduced to simple metrics on a dashboard. But holistic leaders redefine KPIs as more than performance measures—they are culture measures. When leaders only measure revenue, efficiency, or cost savings, they inadvertently signal that people and values are secondary. When they also measure trust, engagement, ethical conduct, and internal leadership development, they declare that *how* results are achieved is as important as the results themselves.

Consider two contrasting KPI systems: one organization measures quarterly revenue and customer acquisition. Another measures those same things but also tracks employee trust scores, internal promotion rates, and the percentage of customers who say they would recommend the company to a friend. The second system paints a richer picture of both performance and purpose.

For leaders, reviewing KPIs becomes a leadership act, not just a management task. By asking, *"What do these numbers say about our values?"* leaders align performance with culture. Over time, KPIs that integrate values create organizations that perform strongly without compromising integrity. The message to followers is clear: results matter, but values matter just as much.

Data as Storytelling – And because numbers alone rarely move people, leaders translate data into stories that spark action. Data in its raw form informs, but data framed as a story inspires. Numbers and charts can tell what happened, but without context, they rarely move hearts. Leaders who master data storytelling turn metrics into meaning. They connect statistics to human experiences, allowing teams and stakeholders to see the story behind the numbers. Instead of saying, *"Engagement increased by 12% this quarter,"* a leader might say, *"That 12% means 150 more people who feel proud to work here and who are bringing their best ideas to the table."* Suddenly, data becomes personal and compelling.

Storytelling with data requires three steps:
1. **Contextualize the numbers.** Place them within a narrative arc—why they matter, what caused the change, and what they mean for the future.
2. **Humanize the impact.** Connect the numbers to real people, whether employees, customers, or communities. This bridges the head and the heart.
3. **Call to action.** Use the story to invite the audience to act—whether doubling down on a success, correcting a course, or investing in a new priority.

When leaders frame data this way, dashboards become more than reports—they become catalysts for change. Employees see themselves in the story, stakeholders understand the stakes, and communities feel included in the progress. Over time, leaders remembered for telling powerful stories with data are the ones whose influence extended beyond the spreadsheet. Their legacy is not just measured in percentages but in the lasting commitments and cultures those stories inspired. And when story meets system, leaders can sustain five simple habits.

Five Practices of Visionary Strategic Leaders

Across contexts, visionary strategic leaders share five habits that keep the future visible and the present accountable.

1. Repeat the vision often until it becomes embedded.
2. Align team goals directly to long-term vision.
3. Use data not just to report, but to inspire and reveal stories.
4. Empower others to take ownership of the vision.
5. Model consistency: Let your actions reinforce what you articulate.

Leaders should not wait for perfect conditions to practice vision casting. Begin where you are. Even in the smallest team or project, the discipline of aligning daily work with a larger purpose trains both leader and team to think beyond the immediate. Habits should show up in evidence, not just effort.

Measuring Strategic Impact

Habits matter most when they produce evidence. Measuring impact proves that the strategy is creating value without sacrificing values. Legacy cannot be claimed; it must be demonstrated. Strategic leaders measure both results and process.

- **Leading indicators:** engagement, innovation, learning velocity.
- **Lagging indicators:** retention, revenue, community impact.

A quarterly **Legacy Summary** provides a snapshot: which values were upheld, which people were developed, which practices were institutionalized. Paired with the Integrity Ledger™, it gives evidence that legacy is more than aspiration—it is action. *Data keeps us honest—so do the patterns that trip most leaders.*

Pitfalls & Best Practices

Even with good intent, leaders stumble in predictable ways. Naming the pitfalls—and the counter-moves—keeps strategy honest.

Pitfall 1: Confusing Activity with Strategy
- Example: Filling calendars with meetings and initiatives without clarifying direction.
- Best Practice: Slow down to clarify vision before launching into execution.

Pitfall 2: Casting Vision Once and Forgetting It
- Example: Sharing a vision statement at a retreat, then never revisiting it.
- Best Practice: Revisit and re-communicate the vision until it becomes culture.

Pitfall 3: Choosing Speed Over Sustainability
- Example: Rushing a project to meet deadlines, even if it compromises values.
- Best Practice: Ask, "Will this decision matter in 10 years?" Legacy requires patience.

Pitfall 4: Leading Alone
- Example: Writing a vision in isolation without input from diverse voices.
- Best Practice: Involve others in shaping vision so ownership spreads.

Pitfall 5: Overpromising Outcomes
- Example: Announcing bold goals without realistic paths.
- Best Practice: Inspire boldly but ground vision in credible action steps.

Reflective Questions

Before you move on, pause. Reflection turns experience into insight and insight into practice.

1. What is your current strategic vision, and how clearly is it communicated?
2. In what ways are your leadership decisions anchored in your values?
3. What ethical dilemmas have you encountered, and how were they resolved?
4. How do you measure alignment between your strategic intent and your organizational culture?

Journaling Prompts
- Reflect on a decision you made that aligned with your values, even when it was costly.
- Journal about how your vision connects to the legacy you want to leave.
- Complete the Strategic Vision Template with your team.
- Begin an Integrity Ledger™ this week.

90-Day Strategic Vision Plan

To lock this in, here's a simple 90-day plan that converts the chapter's ideas into momentum you can see.

Month 1 – Clarify and Communicate
- Write or refine your personal leadership vision.
- Share it with your team and ask for input.

Month 2 – Align and Apply
- Conduct a SWOT analysis.
- Align at least one project directly to your vision and values.

Month 3 – Sustain and Embed
- Revisit the vision with your team.
- Celebrate a milestone that demonstrates progress toward it.
- Document one practice that anchors vision into culture.

Vision and Legacy

Strategy becomes legacy when today's choices echo tomorrow. The final word of this chapter is an invitation—and a charge. Strategic leadership is more than planning—it's courage, ethics, and adaptability in motion. By aligning mission, values, and long-term vision, leaders can shape the future rather than react to it. Every decision becomes a seed of legacy, planted today to be reaped tomorrow. When you cast vision rooted in values and lived in daily choices, you are not just leading for today's outcomes. You are planting seeds that will grow into the legacy of tomorrow.

Your legacy starts with the step you take today. Choose to lead with intention, vision, and integrity. Plans don't persuade—people do. Strategy becomes a shared reality when we communicate with purpose, show up with presence, and keep a steady rhythm. Lead the next decision like it will be remembered—and then repeat the rhythm.

4 COMMUNICATING IMPACT

Leadership lives or dies in communication. You can have the clearest vision, the deepest values, and the strongest strategy, but if you cannot communicate with them in a way that builds trust and inspires action, they will never take root. Communication is the hinge that turns vision into reality, values into culture, and strategy into action. Without it, even the best ideas remain locked inside leaders' heads.

Why Communication is the Lifeblood of Leadership
If leadership is influence, then communication is the bloodstream through which that influence flows. Communication is the vehicle by which vision is cast, trust is cultivated, and conflict is navigated.

Communication is complex, irreversible, and involves the total personality. It carries the weight of organizational purpose and culture. It is not only about what is said but also how, when, and in what spirit it is delivered. Leaders must therefore commit to clarity, authenticity, and alignment between their words and their values.

Good leadership communication depends upon consistency, frequency, and constancy. Effective leaders speak firmly and often, reinforcing priorities with steady messaging. Their words echo because their actions mirror what they say. This integrity is the foundation of credibility. Having established why communication matters, we now turn to what makes leadership communication distinct from everyday conversation.

Holistic leaders go beyond transactional communication. They recognize that every interaction, whether a team meeting, a one-on-one coaching session, or a public address, has the power to shape culture. They avoid manipulation, intimidation, or excessive jargon. Instead, they prioritize clarity, transparency, and respect.

I have found this to be true in my own leadership. When leading a workgroup through a challenging project, I realized quickly that no one was lacking skill — the real barrier was communication. People didn't understand priorities. They weren't sure if their voices mattered. I began to shift the conversation: repeating the vision in every meeting, inviting contributions from each member, and checking in one-on-one to ensure alignment. The change was immediate. Where there had been confusion, there was now confidence. That experience reinforced for me: communication is not a side task of leadership; it is the core. This illustrates a broader truth: clarity is not just about transmitting facts but about reinforcing trust.

Defining Effective Leadership Communication

Effective leadership communication is more than transmitting information; it is about transforming understanding and inspiring action. It requires both substance and style. Every message is received in the context of competing priorities, personal biases, and organizational noise. Effective leaders recognize that communication is not measured by what is spoken, but by what is understood and acted upon.

The goal of leadership communication is to make sure that everyone understands the organization's challenges and what each person must do to promote success. This is not simply about cascading directives from the top down. It is about creating alignment across levels, ensuring that people see where they fit, why their contributions matter, and how their work connects to the broader mission.

Communication must therefore be planned and intentional, ensuring that the message is clear, the delivery consistent, and the frequency sufficient for reinforcement. Random updates, inconsistent talking points, or vague instructions do more harm than silence—they breed uncertainty, which in turn erodes trust. Planned, disciplined communication creates stability and ensures that values and strategy are continually reinforced in both words and actions. Defining communication is the first step; practicing it consistently is where leaders often stumble. To avoid that, let's explore five dimensions that shape communication with impact.

The Five Dimensions of Effective Leadership Communication

1. Clarity of Purpose: Clarity of purpose is the foundation of effective leadership communication. It means moving beyond instructions or directives to articulate why a decision, project, or initiative matters. Without purpose, communication feels transactional; with purpose, it becomes transformational. Purpose elevates even routine updates into opportunities to reinforce values and direction. Leaders who master clarity consistently connect messages to the broader mission, ensuring that people do not just know what to do but understand why it is essential and how it contributes to the legacy being built.

2. Consistency of Message: Consistency signals credibility. When leaders repeat themes across multiple platforms—meetings, written updates, informal conversations—they reinforce priorities and reduce confusion. Inconsistency, by contrast, undermines trust and creates disengagement. Consistency does not mean rigid repetition; it means weaving the same guiding principles into different contexts so that messages are recognizable and trustworthy. Over time, consistency builds organizational rhythm. People come to expect alignment between leadership's words and actions, which strengthens stability and confidence even in times of change.

3. Emotional Resonance: Effective communication does not stop at logic; it must reach the emotional core of people. Emotional resonance means speaking in ways that connect with the hopes, concerns, and aspirations of those being led. Leaders who communicate with emotional resonance acknowledge the realities their teams face while also inspiring belief in the future. It is this blend of empathy and vision that motivates people to go beyond compliance and into commitment. Messages that resonate emotionally are remembered, repeated, and acted upon because they touch both the mind and the heart.

4. Dialogue Orientation: Communication in leadership is not a one-way broadcast but an ongoing dialogue. Dialogue orientation requires leaders to create spaces for questions, feedback, and honest conversation. It reframes communication as collaborative sense-making rather than top-down instruction. Leaders who foster dialogue signal that communication is not about controlling narratives but about co-creating understanding. This orientation not only increases buy-in but also surfaces insights that would remain hidden without reciprocal exchange. In practice, dialogue transforms communication from a monologue into a relationship, where both leaders and followers continually shape meaning.

5. Cultural Sensitivity: Cultural sensitivity ensures that communication honors the diversity of the audience. What inspires one group may alienate another if cultural context is ignored. Leaders must recognize that their words carry different weight depending on background, role, or experience. Cultural sensitivity requires attentiveness to language, symbols, and assumptions that could exclude or diminish people. It also demands an intentional effort to include perspectives that might otherwise be overlooked. Leaders who communicate with cultural sensitivity build credibility across boundaries, creating environments where people feel respected and seen. This inclusivity strengthens cohesion and reinforces the leader's legacy as one who led with both conviction and care.

Pulling It Together: When these five elements—clarity of purpose, consistency of message, emotional resonance, dialogue orientation, and cultural sensitivity—are integrated, leadership communication moves beyond information transfer to transformation. Authenticity is the thread that binds them together. Leaders who communicate authentically admit what they know, acknowledge what they do not, and remain transparent about both successes and setbacks.

The result is communication that does more than instruct—it inspires. People do not merely follow directions; they gain understanding, ownership, and motivation. Over time, communication grounded in these five dimensions creates trust, alignment, and a culture where words and actions reinforce one another.

Practicing Communication with Purpose

I once facilitated a group that had grown frustrated with the lack of progress. Meetings were tense, updates were vague, and trust was beginning to erode. My instinct was to provide more data, more charts, more technical explanations. But as I looked around the room, I realized information wasn't the problem — people were craving meaning.

So I shifted my approach. Instead of starting with the technical details, I began the meeting with a vision: "This isn't just about getting this project across the finish line. This is about creating a model that will make things easier for all of us in the long run. It's about laying groundwork for the next generation of leaders who will carry this forward."

The energy in the room shifted immediately. Faces lifted. Conversations grew more engaged. By reconnecting the group to purpose, I didn't just share information; I ignited commitment. That day taught me that effective leadership communication begins not with data but with meaning. Ask yourself: when was the last time I framed an update in terms of purpose rather than process?

Why Purpose Changes Everything

Purpose reframes communication from a transactional activity into a transformational one. Without purpose, updates sound like obligations—tasks to be completed, deadlines to be met. With purpose, the same updates become part of a larger story. People want to feel that their work matters, that they are contributing to something bigger than themselves. When leaders anchor communication in purpose, they transform routine conversations into moments of inspiration.

In this way, purpose is not a garnish to add at the end of communication; it is the main ingredient. Charts, graphs, and data points may provide clarity, but purpose provides fuel. People are not motivated by spreadsheets—they are motivated by vision, values, and the sense that their efforts have lasting meaning.

Lessons for Leaders
Several lessons emerge from this experience:
1. **Start with the "Why."** Leaders should begin important meetings and communications by connecting people to purpose. This doesn't mean abandoning data—it means framing data within a larger context.
2. **Recognize the Emotional Climate.** When teams are weary, anxious, or discouraged, information alone rarely shifts morale. Leaders must first speak to the more profound need for hope, meaning, and belonging.
3. **Make Purpose Tangible.** Purpose should not remain abstract. Tie it to the lived reality of your team: How will this project make their work easier? How will it improve the lives of those they serve? How will it shape the culture for future leaders?
4. **Use Story as a Vehicle.** Stories, metaphors, and images carry purpose more powerfully than bullet points. By telling a story of where the team is headed, leaders give people something to imagine and believe in.

The Broader Implication

What I learned in that room is something every leader must practice: communication is never just about what we *say*; it is about what people *hear* and how it resonates with their sense of purpose. When leaders fail to connect communication to meaning, people tune out, even if the information is accurate. When leaders succeed in framing communication around purpose, people lean in, commit, and carry the vision forward.

The Discipline of Listening

Listening is the most underutilized leadership tool — and the most powerful. Leaders often believe their authority is measured by how much they speak. In reality, it is measured by how deeply they listen. The leader who dominates every conversation may project confidence, but the leader who listens with intention projects respect, wisdom, and strength.

True listening is not passive. It is an active discipline that requires focus, humility, and patience. Leaders who listen well understand that people long to be heard and that being heard is the first step toward being valued. When leaders neglect listening, they send the subtle message that voices don't matter. When they practice it, they cultivate trust, spark engagement, and open the door to innovation.

I practice active listening by maintaining eye contact, taking notes, and asking clarifying questions. When I sense someone is holding back, I create space by asking: "What's on your mind that we haven't heard yet?" That question signals curiosity and care. It creates a safe place for people to speak candidly, and often the most important insights emerge in response.

During one workgroup session, a member resisted the direction we were taking. Instead of pressing harder, I invited them to share fully while I listened without interruption. I summarized their concerns to ensure I understood correctly. Their posture softened. From that point forward, they contributed more constructively. Listening turned potential resistance into engagement. This reminded me that people are more likely to support what they help shape, and listening is the bridge that allows participation to turn into ownership.

Why Listening Matters in Leadership

Listening is more than a courtesy; it is a strategic practice. It strengthens leaders in three crucial ways:
1. **It builds credibility.** When people feel heard, they are more likely to trust the leader's decisions—even when they disagree with the outcome. Trust grows not because every idea is adopted, but because every idea is acknowledged.
2. **It reveals blind spots.** Leaders who dominate conversations only hear themselves. Leaders who listen invite perspectives that illuminate weaknesses, risks, and opportunities they might otherwise miss.
3. **It creates ownership.** When people are heard, they invest more deeply. Listening communicates, *"Your perspective matters here."* That simple affirmation fuels commitment to the shared vision.

Listening as a Discipline

The challenge for most leaders is not knowing *how* to listen, but choosing to listen when it is inconvenient, uncomfortable, or time-consuming. That is why listening must be treated as a discipline. It requires intentionality and self-control. The temptation will always be to speak quickly, defend positions, or fill silence with more words. But the leader who embraces listening as a discipline recognizes that silence often speaks louder than speech.

A disciplined listener creates space where people feel safe to tell the truth. That truth—whether praise, critique, or insight—equips the leader to lead with greater wisdom. Over time, consistent listening reshapes culture. Meetings shift from performance reviews to authentic dialogue. Resistance transforms into partnership. Followers learn that their voices matter, and leaders discover that the collective wisdom of the group far exceeds the limits of a single perspective.

The Role of Clarity

Ambiguity undermines leadership. Leaders who communicate vaguely leave teams to fill gaps with assumptions, which often breed anxiety.

I make it a discipline to prepare intentionally before high-stakes conversations. I ask myself: *"What do I want them to know? What do I want them to feel? What do I want them to do?"* This simple three-part filter keeps me focused and prevents wasted words.

The best communicators are not those who speak the loudest but those who listen the deepest. Influence is built less through words spoken than through people feeling heard.

Communication in Crisis

Crisis magnifies communication. What may seem like small gaps or inconsistencies in ordinary times become glaring in moments of uncertainty. Followers look to leaders not only for information but also for emotional guidance. In the absence of clarity, rumors fill the void. In the absence of a steady presence, fear takes root.

In a crisis project I led, misinformation was spreading quickly, and anxiety was rising. I gathered the group and spoke plainly: "Here's what we know. Here's what we don't know yet. Here's what we're doing next." By admitting the unknowns while providing direction, I created trust. People don't expect leaders to know everything — but they do expect honesty.

That moment reminded me that in times of crisis, followers are not measuring leaders by their perfection but by their presence. Clear communication steadies people; evasive communication destabilizes them. Even when leaders cannot provide all the answers, they can provide candor, consistency, and calm.

Why Communication Matters More in Crisis

1. **Information Shapes Emotion.** In a vacuum, fear multiplies. When leaders communicate quickly and clearly, they reduce the power of speculation.
2. **Tone Signals Stability.** People mirror the emotional state of their leaders. A leader who speaks with composure creates calm, even if the situation is uncertain.
3. **Honesty Builds Trust.** Followers can accept uncertainty if they are confident that leaders are not hiding the truth. Trust is not built by pretending to have all the answers but by being transparent about what is known and unknown.

Practices for Crisis Communication
- **Lead with transparency.** Say what you know, what you don't know, and what you're doing to find out more.
- **Set a rhythm of updates.** Even if no new information is available, communicate regularly so people aren't left guessing.
- **Balance facts with empathy.** Acknowledge the emotional toll while offering practical next steps.
- **Model composure.** Speak with a steady tone, measured pace, and calm presence. People often remember *how* leaders communicated even more than *what* they communicated.
- **Invite questions.** Allow space for concerns and clarify misinformation quickly before it spreads.

These practices ensure that followers are not only informed but also emotionally steadied—an essential ingredient of legacy leadership.

The Leader's Presence in Crisis

Crisis communication is not only about words—it is about presence. People read body language, tone, and demeanor for cues about whether they are safe. A leader who panics communicates instability, even if their words are technically correct. A leader who is steady communicates confidence, even in uncertainty.

Practicing clarity and composure in crisis turns uncertainty into stability. When leaders combine honesty with empathy, they transform chaotic moments into opportunities for trust to deepen and for culture to strengthen. A crisis may reveal weaknesses in systems, but it also reveals strengths in leadership. Having established principles, leaders now need tools. Frameworks provide practical handles to embody the values of clarity, empathy, and respect.

Frameworks for Effective Communication

Active Listening Model (SOLER): The Active Listening Model, often remembered through the acronym **SOLER**, provides leaders with a practical posture for presence in every conversation. It reminds us that listening is not passive—it is an active discipline that communicates value to the other person before a word is even spoken.

- **S – Sit squarely.** Position your body to face the other person directly. This simple act signals that they have your full attention and that the conversation matters. Leaders who lean away or multitask send the opposite message: *"You are an interruption."*
- **O – Open posture.** Crossed arms or tense shoulders communicate defensiveness, even if unintended. An open posture demonstrates receptivity and respect. It creates a safe space for honesty.
- **L – Lean forward.** A slight lean communicates interest and engagement. It tells the speaker, *"I am here with you, not just in the room."* This physical cue builds trust and rapport.
- **E – Eye contact.** Appropriate, steady eye contact conveys confidence and care. It assures the other person that they are seen and heard. Balanced eye contact avoids distraction without intimidating.
- **R – Relax.** Perhaps the most overlooked element, relaxation ensures that your presence is calm, approachable, and genuine. A relaxed leader communicates safety, making it easier for others to share openly.

When practiced together, SOLER transforms routine conversations into moments of connection. It shows followers that their leader values not only the message but also the person delivering it. Over time, consistent active listening builds loyalty, reduces misunderstandings, and fosters a culture of empathy. The legacy it leaves is profound: a team that knows its voices matter because its leader chose to listen with intention.

Nonviolent Communication: When a conversation is tense, I turn to Marshall Rosenberg's NVC as a checklist for respect: *What did I see? What did I feel? What do we need? What am I asking for?* That sequence lowers defenses and raises clarity. At its core, it shifts dialogue away from blame and accusation and toward empathy and mutual understanding. Instead of escalating tension, NVC creates space for resolution and connection.

The model is built on four elements:
1. **Observations.** Begin by stating the facts without judgment or interpretation. Instead of saying, *"You're always disrespectful in meetings,"* a leader might say, *"In yesterday's meeting, I noticed you spoke while two others were still presenting."* By focusing on observable behavior, leaders prevent defensiveness.
2. **Feelings.** Next, share the emotion connected to the observation. This humanizes the message. For example: *"When that happened, I felt frustrated and concerned."* Naming feelings openly models vulnerability and clarity.
3. **Needs.** Identify the underlying need that connects to the feeling. *"I need to ensure that everyone feels heard so we maintain trust and collaboration on the team."* By stating needs, leaders highlight shared values rather than personal grievances.
4. **Requests.** Finally, make an explicit, actionable request. *"Would you be willing to wait until presenters finish before offering your perspective?"* Requests invite dialogue and change, while demands close doors.

When practiced consistently, NVC transforms conflict into collaboration. It allows leaders to hold others accountable without sacrificing dignity. It is especially powerful in high-stakes environments, cross-cultural teams, or emotionally charged moments where clarity and respect are equally important.

Leaders who embrace NVC leave behind more than resolved conflicts—they leave a culture of communication grounded in empathy and trust. Their legacy is not just what they achieved, but how they spoke, listened, and built bridges when conversations were hardest.

Feedback Framework (SBI – Situation, Behavior, Impact): The SBI Feedback Model—Situation, Behavior, Impact—is one of the simplest and most effective frameworks for giving feedback that is both clear and respectful. Many leaders shy away from feedback because they fear damaging relationships or sparking defensiveness. SBI solves this by grounding conversations in observable facts and their consequences rather than in labels, judgments, or assumptions.
- **Situation.** Begin by naming the specific context. *"In yesterday's client meeting…"*
- **Behavior.** State the actual behavior observed. *"…when you interrupted twice…"*
- **Impact.** Describe the effect that the behavior had. *"…the client disengaged and stopped contributing."*

Conflict Styles (Thomas-Kilmann Model): Conflict is inevitable in any team or organization, but how leaders handle conflict defines both culture and legacy. The Thomas-Kilmann Conflict Mode Instrument identifies five common approaches:
1. **Competing**
2. **Avoiding**
3. **Accommodating**
4. **Compromising**
5. **Collaborating**

Leaders who understand their default conflict style can adapt more intentionally to the situation at hand. For example, a leader who typically avoids conflict might need to lean into collaboration when facing a mission-critical issue. By modeling flexibility and self-awareness, leaders show their teams that conflict is not a threat to unity but an opportunity for growth. Over time, the way leaders navigate conflict becomes part of their legacy—proof that disagreement can deepen trust rather than fracture it.

Conflict Management Styles

Conflict Management styles describe the balance leaders strike between assertiveness (pursuing their own needs or goals) and cooperativeness (addressing the needs or goals of others). No style is inherently right or wrong; each has strengths and risks. The key for leaders is not to default to one style but to discern which approach best fits the situation.

1. Competing: Assertive and uncooperative, the competing style emphasizes winning. It is most useful in emergencies, when quick, decisive action is necessary and there is little time for consensus-building—for example, in safety situations, compliance crises, or critical deadlines. However, used too often, competing breeds resentment and damages trust. Followers may comply outwardly but disengage inwardly.

Leadership Insight: Competing should be a scalpel, not a hammer—reserved for situations where the cost of delay is greater than the cost of relational strain.

2. Accommodating: Cooperative and unassertive, accommodating prioritizes the needs of others over one's own. It can preserve peace and build goodwill in relationships, especially when the issue at hand is minor to the leader but significant to others. However, chronic accommodation risks neglecting essential needs and can create cultures where important concerns are never voiced.

Leadership Insight: Accommodating demonstrates humility and flexibility, but leaders must guard against becoming invisible or enabling unhealthy dynamics.

3. Avoiding: Neither assertive nor cooperative, avoiding conflict altogether. At times, this is wise—when emotions are too high to engage productively, or when the issue is truly insignificant. But avoidance often delays resolution and allows problems to fester, sometimes worsening them. Followers usually interpret avoidance as indifference.

Leadership Insight: Avoidance may buy time, but it rarely buys progress. Leaders should use it as a temporary pause, not a permanent escape.

4. Compromising

Moderately assertive and cooperative, compromising seeks the middle ground. It provides a quick, fair resolution when both parties are willing to give up something. Compromise can be practical, especially when time is limited, but it may also leave both parties partially dissatisfied.

Leadership Insight: Compromise is best when fairness matters more than completeness—such as dividing resources, negotiating schedules, or resolving short-term disputes. But leaders should recognize its limitations: compromise may resolve the issue, but not necessarily strengthen relationships.

5. Collaborating: Highly assertive and highly cooperative, collaborating seeks win-win solutions that honor both sets of needs. It requires time, trust, and creativity, but it produces the most sustainable outcomes. Collaborating moves beyond "splitting the difference" and instead asks: *How can we create a solution that satisfies both sides fully?*

Leadership Insight: Collaboration is the gold standard for holistic leaders. It not only resolves the issue but also deepens trust, builds shared ownership, and reinforces culture. However, it requires patience and a willingness to embrace complexity.

Storytelling as Leadership: Storytelling is one of the oldest leadership tools in human history, and it remains one of the most powerful. Facts inform, but stories inspire. When leaders wrap vision and values in a narrative, they move people not just to understand but to care and to act.

Effective leadership storytelling follows a simple pattern:
- **The context.** Where we are now.
- **The challenge.** What stands in our way?
- **The possibility.** What we can achieve together.
- **The call.** What each person can do to help make it real.

For example, instead of saying, *"We need to improve customer service by 15%,"* a leader might tell the story of one customer who almost left but stayed because of an employee's care and initiative. That story makes the abstract metric tangible and personal.

Storytelling also humanizes leaders. By sharing their own experiences of failure, resilience, or vision, they invite people to connect with them as fellow travelers, not distant authorities. Done well, storytelling becomes a thread that ties vision to daily action. Leaders remembered for their stories are those who gave meaning to the work and identity to the culture. Their legacy endures in the narratives teams tell long after the leader has moved on.

Conflict as Opportunity

Conflict is not the opposite of communication; it is the test of communication. When leaders communicate well in conflict, they demonstrate clarity, empathy, and courage. Conflict is inevitable when people collaborate. The question is not whether it will happen, but how leaders respond. When avoided, conflict festers. Mishandled, it divides. But embraced wisely, it becomes a source of growth.

In a workgroup divided over a key decision, voices grew louder and frustration mounted. Instead of shutting the discussion down, I reframed the conflict: "The fact that you're passionate tells me this matters deeply. Let's treat this as an opportunity to get to the heart of what we value." That shift transformed hostility into dialogue. Conflict, when honored, became fuel for creativity.

Why Leaders Must Reframe Conflict

Conflict reveals what people care about most. Disagreements surface when values, priorities, or perspectives collide. Leaders who see conflict only as disruption miss its deeper purpose: conflict is energy. That energy can destroy trust if ignored or misused, but when harnessed, it becomes momentum for innovation, alignment, and stronger relationships.

When leaders reframe conflict as an opportunity, they:
- Shift the narrative from *"something is wrong"* to *"something important is at stake."*
- Signal that passion is welcome, not punished.
- Open the door for dialogue that clarifies values and strengthens unity.

Practices for Navigating Conflict as Opportunity
1. **Acknowledge, Don't Avoid.** Pretending conflict isn't there only deepens resentment. Leaders must name the tension in the room and legitimize it as something worth addressing.
2. **Reframe Emotion as Investment.** Anger or frustration often signals deep commitment. Leaders can validate the emotion while redirecting it toward constructive dialogue.
3. **Clarify Shared Purpose.** In conflict, people often focus on differences. Leaders should continually bring the group back to what unites them: the mission, the values, and the long-term vision.
4. **Facilitate Dialogue, Not Debate.** Conflict resolution is not about winners and losers; it is about creating shared understanding. Leaders should encourage listening, paraphrasing, and seeking common ground.
5. **Transform Outcomes into Action.** Once conflict produces clarity, leaders must translate that clarity into the next steps. Without action, conflict feels wasted, and cynicism returns.

The Leader's Role in Conflict

Leaders set the tone for how conflict is experienced. A defensive leader escalates tension; a calm leader de-escalates it. A leader who silences disagreement communicates fear; a leader who invites dialogue communicates trust. Ultimately, leaders model whether conflict is destructive or developmental.

When leaders embrace conflict with curiosity and courage, they cultivate cultures where disagreements are not feared but valued. In such cultures, teams learn that tension is not a threat to unity but a pathway to stronger unity.

Why It Matters

Conflict tests communication because it requires leaders to balance truth and grace, assertiveness and empathy. How a leader navigates conflict often becomes one of the most defining aspects of their legacy. Followers rarely forget how a leader handled the most challenging conversations.

By treating conflict as an opportunity, leaders turn moments of division into moments of growth. They model that even when passions run high, values and vision can guide dialogue. In doing so, they transform conflict from a liability into an asset—fuel for trust, creativity, and resilience.

Holistic Leadership and Conflict

Holistic leaders lean toward collaboration because it aligns with the values of trust, respect, and shared growth. But they also understand that no single style works in every context. The art of conflict management is discernment—knowing when to be decisive, when to yield, when to delay, when to compromise, and when to collaborate.

Holistic leaders:
- Choose the style that fits the moment while staying true to values.
- Remain aware of their default style and its impact on others.
- Use conflict as an opportunity to reinforce culture, not just to resolve disputes.

Why It Matters

Conflict management styles are not just academic categories; they are practical choices leaders make every day. Each choice signals something to the team: *Do I care about results? Do I care about relationships? Do I care about both?* Over time, the consistent use of one style shapes culture.

Legacy-minded leaders are remembered not only for what they achieved but also for how they handled conflict along the way. Choosing wisely in conflict demonstrates maturity, strengthens relationships, and transforms tension into trust.

From Theory to Practice

Communication and conflict management are not abstract theories; they are skills that must be embodied daily. Leaders who intentionally practice them cultivate cultures where dialogue is safe, respectful, and productive.

Five Practices for Daily Leadership

Holistic leadership is not built in rare moments of inspiration but in the ordinary rhythms of daily communication. What leaders choose to say, how they choose to listen, and the respect they demonstrate in every interaction accumulate over time into a culture. These five practices are deceptively simple, but when embedded consistently, they transform everyday leadership into legacy. These daily disciplines are the bridge between theory and culture. They move communication from principle to practice.

1. Prepare Messages Intentionally

Communication should never be left to chance. Leaders who enter meetings or conversations without preparation risk sending mixed signals, overlooking important details, or speaking in ways that confuse rather than clarify. Preparing intentionally means deciding in advance not only *what* to communicate, but also *how* it should land.

Ask yourself before every important interaction:
- *What do I want people to know?* (the facts, context, or updates)
- *What do I want people to feel?* (confidence, urgency, reassurance, hope)
- *What do I want people to do?* (the clear action step or commitment)

This simple triad—*know, feel, do*—keeps communication purposeful. It ensures that leaders go beyond information dumping to inspire understanding and action. Anticipating possible misunderstandings also allows leaders to clarify proactively, preventing confusion before it takes root.

2. Practice Active Listening

Listening is not the pause between speaking; it is an act of leadership in itself. Practicing active listening means creating space for others to share fully before responding. Leaders who cut people off, rush to conclusions, or focus only on their own rebuttals erode trust. Leaders who listen deeply send the message: *Your perspective matters here.*

Practical disciplines include:
- Waiting until the other person has fully finished before speaking.
- Paraphrasing what you heard: *"What I hear you saying is…"*
- Checking for accuracy: *"Did I capture that correctly?"*

Active listening requires patience, but its impact is powerful. People who feel heard are more likely to engage constructively, even in disagreement. Over time, this discipline fosters a culture where dialogue is valued over debate and collaboration over competition.

3. Invite Feedback Regularly

Feedback should not be reserved for annual reviews or formal surveys. Holistic leaders weave feedback into everyday interactions so it becomes a natural rhythm rather than an intimidating event. This normalizes growth and communicates humility: leaders who ask for feedback show they are still learning.

Questions can be short and simple:
- *"What's one way I can improve communication with you?"*
- *"How could I have led that meeting more effectively?"*

When feedback is invited regularly, people stop seeing it as criticism and start seeing it as collaboration. Leaders also gain real-time insights that allow for quick adjustments instead of waiting until minor frustrations become significant problems.

4. Model Respect Consistently

Respect is one of the clearest signals of leadership integrity. It shows up in tone, body language, and the willingness to acknowledge perspectives that differ from your own. Leaders set the standard: if they remain calm and constructive in disagreement, teams learn to do the same. If they dismiss or belittle others, disrespect spreads.

Practical ways to model respect include:
- Keeping tone steady and words constructive, even in conflict.
- Acknowledging opposing views: *"I see the point you're making, and here's how I'm processing it."*
- Thanking people for raising difficult questions instead of punishing dissent.

Respect demonstrated in daily moments builds psychological safety—the sense that people can speak honestly without fear. That safety, in turn, fuels innovation and trust.

5. Debrief Conflict and Capture Lessons

Conflict does not end when tempers cool or decisions are made. If leaders fail to process conflict afterward, valuable lessons are lost, and patterns repeat. Debriefing conflict ensures that teams turn tension into growth.

After a conflict is resolved, take time for reflection:
- Ask: *"What did we learn about ourselves as a team?"*
- Ask: *"What will we do differently next time?"*

Documenting insights ensures they are not forgotten in the rush of daily work. Over time, these lessons can be codified into team norms, creating a culture where conflict strengthens rather than weakens relationships.

Why These Practices Matter

Individually, these five practices may seem modest. Together, they shape culture. Culture is not built in grand speeches or annual strategy sessions—it is built in the ordinary, repeated actions of leaders. Intentional preparation ensures clarity. Active listening fosters trust. Feedback creates growth. Respect stabilizes relationships. Debriefing conflict turns challenges into learning.

When woven into the daily rhythm of leadership, these practices accumulate. They become the invisible scaffolding that supports a healthy, resilient organization. Followers stop wondering if leaders will listen, communicate clearly, or respect them in disagreement; they come to expect it. That expectation becomes culture. Culture, in turn, becomes the soil where trust, collaboration, and legacy grow.

Holistic leadership is not about dramatic gestures—it is about consistency. It is about small acts of intentionality practiced faithfully until they define both the leader and the team. In this way, ordinary habits give rise to extraordinary legacies.

Applying These Practices

I once closed a project debrief by asking the group to share not only what went well but also what we learned through tension. The answers were profound: they spoke of trust, resilience, and how conflict had sharpened their thinking. Practicing debriefing turned a stressful season into a lasting lesson. What could have been remembered only as a challenging project became a defining moment of growth.

This is what happens when leaders practice daily disciplines. The practices are not theoretical; they shape real experiences and leave lasting imprints on people. Debriefing a conflict transforms it from an uncomfortable memory into a training ground for the future. Listening with patience turns resistance into engagement. Modeling respect in disagreement prevents fractures and preserves dignity. Over time, these habits build credibility.

The Ripple Effect

When leaders practice these habits day after day, people begin to expect fairness, clarity, and respect. Expectations then turn into norms: *This is how we do things here.* New team members adopt the culture quickly because they see it modeled consistently. Conflict is addressed constructively, meetings begin with a purpose, and conversations include feedback loops.

The ripple extends beyond the immediate team. A leader's consistency builds trust with clients, partners, and communities. The way communication is handled inside the organization shapes reputation outside the organization. What begins as five simple practices becomes a leadership legacy that others remember, emulate, and extend.

Lasting Impact

The true test of leadership is not whether people achieve results in the leader's presence, but whether the culture sustains those results in the leader's absence. These daily practices outlast the moment. They teach people how to listen, respect, grow, and resolve conflict even after the leader has moved on. That is the essence of holistic leadership—leaving behind a culture of integrity, trust, and growth that continues to bear fruit.

Pitfalls & Best Practices
Pitfall 1: Speaking More Than Listening
- Example: Dominating meetings and leaving little space for input.
- Best Practice: Practice active listening; aim for at least 50% listening in conversations.

Pitfall 2: Avoiding Difficult Conversations
- Example: Ignoring conflict until it escalates into bigger issues.
- Best Practice: Address issues early with clarity and compassion.

Pitfall 3: Assuming Understanding Without Checking
- Example: Giving directions once and assuming everyone is aligned.
- Best Practice: Ask others to restate what they heard to confirm clarity.

Pitfall 4: Using Communication Only to Inform
- Example: Sharing updates but never inspiring action.
- Best Practice: Use communication to inspire, align, and reinforce culture.

Pitfall 5: Managing Conflict with Power Instead of Dialogue
- Example: Shutting down disagreement by pulling rank.
- Best Practice: Invite open dialogue; conflict well-managed strengthens trust.

Reflective Questions
1. How consistent is your communication with your values?
2. Do you listen to understand, or to respond?
3. How do you typically handle conflict: avoid, compete, accommodate, compromise, or collaborate?
4. What feedback structures exist for your team?
5. How do you model respectful dialogue under pressure?

Journaling Prompts
- Describe a conflict you addressed directly. What difference did it make?
- Reflect on a moment when clarity in communication shifted outcomes.
- Write about a time you practiced listening deeply. How did it change the relationship?
- Journal about how you communicate in times of stress. What does that reveal?
- Write about a recent conversation where listening made a difference.
- Reflect on a time when your communication created a misunderstanding. What would you do differently now?
- Journal about how you handle conflict. Which style do you tend to use, and how does it affect outcomes?

90-Day Communication & Conflict Growth Plan

Month 1 – Listening First
- Prepare intentionally before every high-stakes conversation.
- Practice active listening in one conversation per day.
- Ask two people for feedback on how you communicate.

Month 2 – Speaking with Clarity
- As outlined earlier, the SBI model provides a clear, respectful framework for feedback.
- Reframe one complex idea into a simple, clear message for your team.

Month 3 – Building Culture and Collaboration
- Practice addressing one minor conflict directly and constructively.
- Share one story that connects your team's work to a larger vision.

By the end of 90 days, you will not only communicate more effectively but also model a culture where dialogue is safe, feedback is welcomed, and conflict fuels growth rather than fear.

Communication is the bridge between vision and action. Leaders remembered for their legacy are not only those who dreamed boldly but also those who spoke in ways that shaped culture, built trust, and inspired generations. Words fade, but the trust they create endures. Words align direction; teams deliver it. Communication sets the stage, but without systems to embed it, alignment drifts. The next chapter turns to how leaders cultivate trust through accountability and systems that sustain legacy.

5 BUILDING DYNAMIC TEAMS

No leader builds a legacy alone. Leadership multiplies when it is shared, and the most significant impact comes from teams that are diverse, dynamic, and aligned with purpose. Building teams is not only about productivity; it is about creating communities of trust and resilience that endure beyond the leader. Legacy begins in community, not in isolation. The way leaders build teams determines whether their influence scales or stops with them.

Why Teams Matter
The measure of effective leadership is not only what is accomplished individually but also what is accomplished collectively. Teams amplify capacity, extend influence, and transform vision into action. At their best, teams become more than the sum of their parts — they generate creativity, resilience, and outcomes no individual could have achieved alone.

But great teams do not form by accident. They require intentional cultivation, grounded in diversity, equity, inclusion, and trust. Most importantly, they must be built to thrive in change. A dynamic team does not avoid conflict or resist disruption, but one that adapts, grows, and multiplies its impact.

I have seen the difference between a group that functions merely as individuals and one that operates as a true team. In one project, the early weeks were marked by silos. People worked diligently, but only within their narrow lanes. Progress was slow and innovation minimal. When I shifted the focus to shared goals, encouraged cross-collaboration, and modeled trust, the atmosphere changed. People began volunteering ideas, supporting one another, and thinking beyond their assignments. That team became one of the most effective I have ever led. The lesson was clear: building a dynamic team requires leaders to create conditions where collaboration becomes natural.

This principle—that teams multiply leadership—sets the foundation for exploring how they actually develop and grow.

The Stages of Team Development

Psychologist Bruce Tuckman described five stages of team development:

- **Forming:** Individuals are polite, roles unclear, energy high, but tentative.
- **Storming:** Conflict arises as personalities and priorities clash.
- **Norming:** Patterns develop, roles clarify, trust begins to form.
- **Performing:** The team operates at high efficiency, aligned to purpose.
- **Adjourning:** The team completes its task, celebrates, and disbands or re-forms.

Dynamic teams revisit these stages regularly as new challenges and members arise. Leaders who understand this cycle are better prepared to guide teams through it. Leaders often want to skip storming, but it is essential—healthy conflict is the bridge from surface-level collaboration to genuine trust. I've led groups through storming phases where tension was uncomfortable. But instead of avoiding it, I framed it as a sign of growth. By normalizing conflict, the group emerged stronger and more united. Dynamic teams are not conflict-free; in fact, their strength often emerges through healthy tension. What matters is how leaders frame the challenge and guide the group through it.

Research on team effectiveness consistently points to two core drivers: trust and clarity. Teams thrive when members feel safe to contribute and when they understand the shared goal. Without these, talent is wasted; with them, even average groups can achieve extraordinary results.

Frameworks for Dynamic Teams

As described earlier, Tuckman's stages help leaders anticipate and guide team development.

For leaders, the value lies not in memorizing the labels but in recognizing the signals. A team in storming needs patience, facilitation, and trust-building. A team performing needs protection from unnecessary interference. By naming the stage and leading accordingly, leaders reduce frustration and accelerate progress. Over time, this awareness helps teams view conflict not as dysfunction but as part of growth—a lesson that becomes part of the team's enduring culture.

Psychological Safety (Amy Edmondson): Harvard professor Amy Edmondson defines psychological safety as the shared belief that a team is safe for interpersonal risk-taking. In simple terms, people feel they can speak up without fear of embarrassment, punishment, or exclusion. Teams with high psychological safety innovate more, learn faster, and adapt better—because people are willing to voice half-formed ideas, admit mistakes, or raise concerns.

For leaders, creating psychological safety means modeling humility ("I may be wrong, what do you see?"), rewarding candor, and responding to failure with curiosity rather than blame. A culture of safety does not mean lowering standards; it means raising trust so that high standards can be met collaboratively. Leaders who practice this leave behind more than high-performing teams—they leave a culture where people believe their voice matters, long after the leader has left the room.

Creating psychological safety requires leaders to model vulnerability. Admitting, *"I don't have all the answers, but together we can figure this out,"* signals that imperfection is allowed. Over time, this builds trust and openness.

Diversity & Inclusion Frameworks: Diversity brings a variety of perspectives, experiences, and identities into the team. Inclusion ensures those perspectives are heard, respected, and integrated. Without inclusion, diversity becomes tokenism. With inclusion, diversity becomes strength. Frameworks such as the "Diversity Wheel" or "Inclusion Continuum" remind leaders that identity extends beyond visible differences like race and gender, to include background, thinking styles, and lived experiences.

Leaders build inclusive teams by rotating who facilitates meetings, intentionally seeking out quieter voices, and ensuring credit is shared fairly. Research consistently shows that diverse teams outperform homogenous ones in creativity and decision-making. But beyond performance, inclusive leadership communicates dignity: *you belong here, your contribution matters*. Leaders who embrace diversity and inclusion as more than compliance leave behind teams that see difference not as a barrier but as an advantage. Inclusion is what transforms diversity from a headcount into a heartbeat.

Strengths-Based Leadership: Strengths-based leadership shifts the focus from fixing weaknesses to amplifying strengths. Instead of asking, *"Where are you deficient?"* leaders ask, *"Where do you shine, and how can we build on that?"* Frameworks like Gallup's CliftonStrengths identify natural talents, such as strategic thinking, relationship-building, or execution.

When leaders align tasks with strengths, people gain energy and confidence. A detail-oriented team member thrives when trusted with quality control; a big-picture thinker flourishes when invited into strategy. Of course, weaknesses cannot be ignored, but strengths-based leadership ensures that people spend the majority of their time where they are naturally gifted. Over time, this approach builds momentum, engagement, and loyalty. The legacy left behind is a culture where people feel seen not for what they lack, but for what they bring. When strengths are amplified and weaknesses supported, momentum becomes a sustainable culture.

Adaptive Leadership: Adaptive leadership, developed by Ronald Heifetz and Marty Linsky, emphasizes leading people through change by balancing stability with flexibility. Unlike technical problems, which have clear solutions, adaptive challenges require learning, experimentation, and resilience. For example, implementing a new software system is not just about technology—it's about shifting mindsets, retraining habits, and reimagining workflows.

Adaptive leaders provide enough stability to reassure people of their values and purpose, while offering enough flexibility to navigate uncertainty. They "get on the balcony" to see the bigger picture and resist the urge to provide quick fixes when adaptive work is needed. Instead, they frame challenges honestly, engage the collective wisdom of the team, and support people through the discomfort of change. Leaders who master adaptive leadership leave organizations not only stronger in the moment but more resilient for whatever comes next. Ask yourself: in the last six months, have you provided both stability and stretch for your team?

Emotional Intelligence and Team Resilience

Emotional intelligence (EQ) is one of the most critical competencies for building and sustaining dynamic teams. Research by John Mayer and Daniel Goleman shows that leaders with high EQ are better able to regulate their emotions, read the emotional climate of their teams, and respond with empathy.

In practice, this means leaders can defuse tensions before they fracture relationships and can interpret silence, hesitation, or resistance not as defiance but as signals of unspoken concerns. Teams led by leaders with a high EQ recover faster from setbacks because members feel understood rather than dismissed.

Resilience is not simply a personal trait; it becomes a collective asset when emotional intelligence is practiced across the team. A resilient team:

- Normalizes stress without stigmatizing it.
- Names challenges openly, which reduces anxiety.
- Adapts quickly to change because members trust one another to remain steady.

Holistic leaders cultivate this by modeling vulnerability ("I don't have all the answers, but we will figure it out together") and by coaching members to reflect on how their emotional patterns affect collaboration. The team becomes more than just skilled—it becomes emotionally intelligent as a unit, which equips it to thrive under pressure. Frameworks help leaders recognize the signals of team growth, but recognition alone is not enough. What transforms ordinary groups into resilient teams is the leader's ability to bring emotional intelligence into daily practice. This resilience ensures that teams do not just survive change but grow stronger because of it.

Leading Through Change

Change is inevitable. Markets shift, technologies evolve, teams reorganize, and priorities adapt. The question is never *if* change will come, but *how* leaders and their teams will respond when it does.

Dynamic teams are not those that avoid disruption or cling to the familiar. They are the ones that embrace change with resilience—seeing it not as a threat but as an opportunity to grow, innovate, and redefine what is possible. This requires leaders at every level, not just those at the top, to develop the mindset and skills of a change agent.

For too long, "change management" has been treated as an HR function or a technical process. In reality, guiding people through transition is at the core of leadership itself. Every leader—whether they supervise three people on a service team, manage a department of dozens, or run an entire organization—will face moments when they must help others navigate uncertainty. Change management is not a side responsibility; it is leadership in action.

To lead effectively through change, leaders must master three commitments:

1. **Cast a Clear Vision**
   People can tolerate disruption if they know where they are going and why it matters. Leaders at all levels must be able to say: *"Here's what's changing, here's why, and here's how it connects to our shared mission."* Without this clarity, confusion breeds resistance.

2. **Balance Stability with Flexibility**
   Followers need reassurance that core values and purpose will remain constant even as methods or tools shift. Leaders provide stability by protecting what does not change—identity, mission, and trust—while showing flexibility in adapting practices, processes, or strategies.

3. **Attend to the Human Side of Change**
   Behind every organizational shift are real people facing loss of familiarity, routines, or even confidence. Leaders who acknowledge those emotions and respond with empathy build deeper trust. Resistance is not a sign of weakness; it is often a sign of fear. Wise leaders engage that resistance rather than dismiss it.

Consider the contrast: a supervisor who dismisses concerns with 'this is the new way, get used to it' erodes morale, while one who says, 'I know this is a big adjustment...let's make it work together,' earns trust and resilience. The difference is not the size of the change but the presence of leadership.

At the executive level, leading through change often involves strategy, culture, and systems. At the front line, it may involve shifting a workflow, adopting new technology, or restructuring responsibilities. In both cases, the principles are the same: leaders must frame the change, support their people, and keep the team focused on the larger purpose.

Holistic leaders understand that every change—big or small—presents a chance to shape legacy. How a leader shows up during transition becomes part of how they are remembered. Those who approach change with clarity, empathy, and resilience not only move their teams forward but also leave behind cultures better prepared for the next disruption.

Understanding Change Management

At its simplest, **change management** is the structured approach to moving individuals, teams, and organizations from their current state to a desired future state. But beyond process, it is about people — their emotions, fears, and hopes. Leaders who neglect this reality often find that even the most rational strategies fail.

The research of John Kotter, William Bridges, and the ADKAR model converges on this truth: change succeeds not because of technical plans, but because of human adoption. To make change practical, leaders can draw on proven frameworks. These are not checklists to memorize but lenses for guiding people through transition.

Kotter's 8 Steps: John Kotter's 8-step process remains one of the most influential frameworks for leading organizational change. Each step is designed to create both momentum and staying power:

1. **Create urgency.** Change begins when people feel the need. Leaders generate urgency by naming the risks of inaction and the opportunities of moving forward.
2. **Build a guiding coalition.** No leader drives change alone. Coalitions of credible, committed individuals expand influence and build trust across the organization.
3. **Form a strategic vision.** Clear vision provides direction. It answers, *"What are we changing to, and why?"*
4. **Communicate the vision.** Vision must be repeated consistently and through multiple channels. Leaders embody it in words and actions.
5. **Empower action.** Remove barriers—whether structural, cultural, or procedural—that prevent people from acting on the vision.
6. **Generate short-term wins.** Early victories prove the change is real and worth the effort. They also build confidence and momentum.
7. **Consolidate gains.** Leaders must resist declaring victory too soon. Sustaining change means using momentum to drive more profound transformation.
8. **Anchor in culture.** The change endures only when it becomes part of the organization's DNA—woven into stories, rituals, and values.

Leaders who practice Kotter's steps thoughtfully ensure change is not a flash in the pan but a legacy shift that outlasts them.

Bridges' Transition Model: William Bridges' Transition Model emphasizes that change is situational, but transition is psychological. It focuses not on the mechanics of change but on the human journey through it. The model describes three phases:

1. **Ending, Losing, Letting Go.** Every new beginning requires an ending. People must first acknowledge what is being lost—whether habits, relationships, or identity. Leaders who rush this stage create resistance. Leaders who honor it build trust.

2. **Neutral Zone.** This is the in-between space, when the old is gone but the new is not fully formed. It can feel confusing, uncertain, or unproductive. Yet it is also the fertile ground for creativity and renewal. Leaders guide people through the neutral zone by offering reassurance, structure, and space for experimentation.
3. **New Beginning.** Eventually, people embrace the new reality. Energy rises, roles become clearer, and commitment deepens. Leaders celebrate, reinforce, and model the new behaviors to anchor them.

This model reminds leaders that successful transitions require patience. It is not enough to design a new strategy; leaders must shepherd people through endings, the uncertainty of the middle, and the hope of new beginnings. Doing so creates loyalty and resilience that endure beyond the immediate change.

ADKAR: The ADKAR model, developed by Prosci, provides a people-centered roadmap for individual change. It highlights the building blocks every person needs to move from awareness to adoption:
1. **Awareness.** People must first understand *why* the change is needed. Without awareness, change feels arbitrary.
2. **Desire.** Awareness does not guarantee buy-in. Leaders must spark desire by connecting change to personal and organizational benefits.
3. **Knowledge.** Desire without know-how leads to frustration. Leaders provide training, resources, and clarity so people know *what to do*.
4. **Ability.** Knowledge must be practiced. Leaders create opportunities, coaching, and support so people can demonstrate competence.
5. **Reinforcement.** Change sticks when leaders celebrate wins, recognize adopters, and integrate new behaviors into systems and culture.

ADKAR is especially powerful because it emphasizes the human side of change—meeting people where they are. Leaders who walk teams through these five steps ensure that change is not just mandated but lived, multiplying the chance that it becomes permanent.

When frameworks are woven together, they help leaders lead change with both strategy and empathy, ensuring not just compliance but commitment.

The Emotional Side of Change

Resistance is not irrational; it is profoundly human. People resist change not because they are stubborn or uncommitted, but because change threatens something deeply personal. It often signals loss—loss of control, loss of competence, loss of familiarity, or loss of security. Even when the change is objectively positive, the fear of what might be lost can overshadow the hope of what could be gained.

Leaders at every level—from the frontline supervisor introducing a new shift schedule to the executive driving a global restructuring—must learn to interpret resistance not as disloyalty but as a natural emotional response. This requires empathy, patience, and a willingness to engage with concerns rather than dismiss them.

Why People Resist:
- **Loss of Control:** Change can make people feel powerless, especially if decisions are made without their input.
- **Loss of Competence:** A new process or technology can make capable employees feel suddenly inadequate.
- **Loss of Familiarity:** Old routines carry comfort. New ways of working often trigger discomfort because they disrupt the known.
- **Loss of Security:** Change can create uncertainty about roles, job stability, or future opportunities.

Understanding these dynamics shifts the leader's perspective. Resistance becomes less of a problem to eliminate and more of a signal to engage.

I once led a significant transition where skepticism surfaced in whispers and side conversations. People were polite in meetings but hesitant in practice. Rather than pressing forward with false optimism, I addressed it directly: *"I want to hear your concerns. Let's put them all on the table."* That invitation unlocked honesty. What surfaced were not objections to the change itself but fears of being left behind—fears of not having the skills, knowledge, or support to succeed in the new environment.

When those fears were acknowledged rather than dismissed, the team felt seen. We invested in training, created safe spaces for practice, and reassured them that success would be shared. Ownership shifted from leadership's mandate to the team's mission. Over time, the same individuals who had been most resistant became the strongest advocates because they were included in the journey rather than pushed along it.

For leaders at all levels, the lesson is this: people don't need perfect plans as much as they need reassurance that they won't face change alone. Frontline leaders can provide this through regular check-ins and coaching conversations. Middle managers can provide it by translating organizational vision into practical relevance for their teams. Executives can provide it by modeling transparency and acknowledging the human cost of disruption as much as the strategic benefits.

Change will always have an emotional side. Leaders who attend to it transform resistance into resilience, fear into trust, and skepticism into commitment.

The Leader's Role in Change

A leader's job is not to eliminate resistance but to channel it into growth. This requires:

1. **Vision Casting** – Communicate the "why" clearly and repeatedly.
2. **Listening** – Surface fears without judgment.
3. **Equipping** – Provide tools, training, and support.
4. **Modeling** – Demonstrate adaptability personally.
5. **Celebrating** – Recognize progress and reinforce momentum.

I once led a group that was visibly fatigued from constant transitions. I made it a point to acknowledge their weariness before outlining the next phase: *"I know this is stretching us, and I see the effort you're giving. Here's how we're going to make it manageable, together."* The honesty built trust, and the vision gave them renewed focus. These commitments turn disruption into development. Without them, change fractures trust; with them, change builds legacy.

Practical Tools for Leading Change
- **Resistance Mapping:** Identify groups likely to support, resist, or stay neutral, then tailor engagement.
- **Feedback Loops:** Schedule regular check-ins to hear concerns and adjust plans.
- **Change Ambassadors:** Empower respected team members to model and advocate for the change.
- **Storytelling:** Share real stories of success that make change tangible.
- **Short-Term Wins:** Celebrate milestones to build belief and momentum.

I have practiced these consistently by empowering "champions" in projects. When peers see colleagues embrace change, it normalizes adaptation far more than any directive from the top. These tools are most effective when modeled consistently, so teams see that change is not just mandated but embodied.

Embedding Change in Culture
Change does not end with implementation. A new system may go live, a reorganization may be announced, or a process may be rolled out, but unless the behaviors that support it are reinforced, teams will drift back to old patterns. Leaders often underestimate this phase, assuming that once training is complete or the announcement is made, the change will "stick." In reality, the true test of leadership begins after the launch.

To embed change, leaders must anchor it in the culture of the team or organization. Culture is not created by policies on paper but by the rhythms, rituals, and reinforcements of everyday life. If old habits are rewarded, celebrated, or tolerated, they will return. If new habits are recognized, celebrated, and aligned with shared values, they become the new normal.

Leaders at every level can help anchor change by:
1. **Modeling the Behavior:** Teams watch leaders closely, especially in the early days of change. A supervisor who uses the new system consistently signals seriousness. An executive who references new priorities in strategic conversations shows alignment from the top.
2. **Reinforcing Through Recognition:** When someone demonstrates the new way of working, celebrate it—publicly and specifically. Recognition not only rewards the individual but also signals to the group that "this is who we are now."
3. **Integrating into Daily Practices:** Leaders must ensure that new processes are embedded into team meetings, performance reviews, and decision-making. For example, if collaboration is the new priority, agendas should highlight cross-team updates, not just siloed reporting.
4. **Aligning Systems and Structures:** If performance metrics, incentives, or policies remain tied to the old way of working, culture will not shift. Leaders must review systems to ensure they reward the desired behaviors.
5. **Telling the Story of Identity:** Change endures when people see it not as an isolated project but as part of their collective identity. Leaders should connect the change to who the group is becoming: *"We are doing this not just because it's new, but because it reflects who we are and the values we stand for."*

I remind groups that embedding change is about transformation, not compliance. Compliance may generate short-term results, but identity creates lasting alignment. When change is linked to values and vision—when people can say, *"This is who we are now"*—it becomes self-sustaining.

Leaders must treat backsliding not as failure but as feedback. Each misstep is an opportunity to reinforce, retrain, and remind the team of the bigger picture. Over time, small, consistent reinforcements shape culture more effectively than one-time announcements or grand gestures.

For frontline leaders, embedding change may look like consistent coaching conversations and celebrating small wins. For middle managers, it may mean aligning departmental goals and processes with the new vision. For executives, it may mean telling the organizational story in ways that make the change inseparable from identity and strategy.

The ultimate goal is this: change becomes less about *what we do differently* and more about *who we are together.* When leaders embed change in culture, they do more than implement a new initiative—they redefine the team's DNA so that progress endures beyond the leader, the project, or the moment.

Developing Leaders Within Teams

A healthy team is more than a collection of capable people; it is a leadership incubator that multiplies influence and prepares the next generation to step forward with confidence.

Leadership is not about titles or positions—it is about influence, responsibility, and the courage to serve others. Every team, no matter its size or context, has members with untapped leadership potential. Some may already show initiative, while others may only need opportunity and encouragement to discover their capacity.

Leaders who intentionally cultivate leadership within their teams do three critical things:

1. **Delegate Authority, Not Just Tasks.** Assigning work is easy; entrusting responsibility is harder. When leaders invite team members to own decisions, not just activities, they communicate trust and create space for growth.
2. **Provide Visible Opportunities.** Rotating who facilitates meetings, who presents progress updates, or who represents the team in cross-functional conversations gives members practice leading in safe, supported contexts.
3. **Build a Mentorship Culture.** Pairing emerging leaders with experienced peers accelerates development and strengthens bonds. Mentorship signals that growth is expected and supported, not reserved for a few.

I have seen hesitant individuals—quiet in meetings, reluctant to speak up—become confident leaders when given the chance to lead a sub-project or mentor a newer teammate. At first, their steps were tentative, but with practice and encouragement, they found their voice. The transformation was visible: the more they led, the more ownership they took, and the more the team flourished because leadership was shared.

For frontline supervisors, this may look like letting a team member run part of a staff meeting. For middle managers, it may mean assigning someone to lead a departmental initiative. For executives, it often involves creating structures—like leadership development programs or succession pipelines—that institutionalize growth. In all cases, the principle is the same: a leader's true legacy is not measured in personal achievement, but in the leaders they leave behind. In every case, the measure of leadership is not what one person achieved but how many leaders they left behind.

From Theory to Practice
Building dynamic teams requires both philosophy and action. It is not enough to talk about trust, collaboration, or empowerment—leaders must translate these values into habits that shape daily culture.

The bridge between theory and practice is discipline: the consistent actions that reinforce identity and expectations. When values are not visible in daily behavior, they fade into slogans. But when leaders embody values in tangible routines, teams internalize them until they become second nature.

Daily Habits of Dynamic Leaders
- **Begin meetings by reconnecting to vision and purpose.** This practice keeps the "why" in front of the "what" and prevents the team from drifting into task-driven fatigue.
- **Create rituals of recognition.** Celebrating effort, creativity, and growth reminds people that progress is more than metrics—it is about becoming better together.
- **Establish ground rules for dialogue.** Protecting respect ensures that disagreement sharpens ideas rather than fractures relationships.
- **Encourage cross-collaboration.** Breaking down silos allows information to flow freely and prevents teams from retreating into isolated lanes.
- **Facilitate team reflections.** Asking questions like, *"What do you think we've learned about ourselves in this process?"* surfaces insights that metrics often miss. Reflection transforms experience into wisdom.

When these habits are practiced consistently, they create an identity where the team itself becomes the legacy. I have found that reflection moments are often the most powerful. In one session, when I asked my team to reflect on what we had learned about ourselves during a difficult project, the responses revealed both hidden strengths and blind spots no one had previously named. That honesty deepened trust, sharpened our identity, and created momentum for the next challenge.

Leaders who build these habits into the culture create teams that are not only effective but transformative. They ensure that theory becomes practice, and practice becomes legacy. Even the best leaders stumble. Anticipating common pitfalls ensures that growth is sustained.

Pitfalls & Best Practices
Pitfall 1: Confusing Harmony with Health
- Example: Believing a lack of disagreement means success.
- Best Practice: Encourage healthy conflict; it leads to stronger solutions.

Pitfall 2: Treating Diversity as Optics
- Example: Hiring for demographics without valuing different perspectives.
- Best Practice: Create structures where all voices are heard and valued.

Pitfall 3: Overcontrolling the Team
- Example: Micromanaging every detail, stifling creativity.
- Best Practice: Empower ownership and celebrate initiative.

Pitfall 4: Neglecting Renewal
- Example: Running from one project to another without pause.
- Best Practice: Build in celebration and reflection rhythms.

Pitfall 5: Failing to Clarify Purpose
- Example: Teams work hard but don't know why.
- Best Practice: Connect daily tasks back to mission and vision.

Reflective Questions
1. How does your team handle conflict during change?
2. Are all voices equally heard and valued?
3. What stage of development is your team in right now?
4. How does your leadership style foster or hinder psychological safety?
5. In what ways are you preparing your team members to lead?
6. How do you approach resistance in times of transition?

Journaling Prompts
- Write about a time your team struggled through conflict but emerged stronger.
- Reflect on whether every voice on your team feels heard.
- Journal about how you celebrate progress and how you could do it more intentionally.

90-Day Team Growth and Change Plan

Month 1 – Building Trust and Inclusion
- Assess current team dynamics and identify gaps.
- Implement structured turn-taking in meetings.
- Create space for anonymous feedback.

Month 2 – Embracing Change and Conflict
- Assign tasks based on individual strengths.
- Share the vision for an upcoming project or initiative and invite honest dialogue.
- Identify likely sources of resistance and engage them directly.

Month 3 – Sustaining Change and Developing Leaders
- Appoint change ambassadors within the team.
- Pair experienced and emerging leaders in mentorship.
- Celebrate one success story that highlights adaptation and growth.

At the end of 90 days, your team will not only function more effectively but also grow as a resilient, adaptive community of leaders, prepared to embrace change as an opportunity.

Dynamic teams carry vision forward long after the leader moves on. When you invest in building resilient, diverse, and trusting groups, you create more than results — you create communities of influence that extend your leadership legacy into the future. Strong teams scale performance; coaching and mentorship scale leaders. That is how cultures outlast any one individual. Dynamic teams sustain momentum, but only if leaders steward trust across the organization. The next chapter explores how credibility and character anchor teams beyond any single season of performance

6 COACHING AND MENTORSHIP

Enduring leaders aren't remembered only for results, but for the people they develop. Coaching sharpens today; mentorship shapes tomorrow. Together, they form the heartbeat of legacy.

The Power of Investing in People

Leadership is not measured solely by the results achieved but by the people developed along the way. The truest legacies are not built through quarterly outcomes or single achievements, but through the leaders who deliberately invest in others, drawing out potential and shaping future influencers. What follows distinguishes coaching from mentorship and shows how to practice both with discipline.

Coaching and mentorship are two of the most powerful ways this investment takes form. Coaching sharpens skills in the present; mentorship shapes vision for the future. Both require time, patience, and intentionality, but both yield returns far greater than any single accomplishment.

A quiet contributor had sharp insights but low confidence. I began asking, 'What do you think?' and gave space to try. Confidence rose, and soon, they led a critical discussion. Growth follows consistent encouragement, specific feedback, and safe practice. That growth didn't happen by accident; it came through consistent encouragement, intentional feedback, and space to practice.

This is the essence of investing in people: creating environments where hidden potential can surface and flourish. Often, individuals underestimate their own capacity until someone else names it, nurtures it, and calls it forth. Leaders who commit to this kind of investment are remembered less for the policies they enforced and more for the people they believed in.

Why Investment Matters at Every Level:
- **Frontline leaders** encourage, teach practical skills, and model integrity in daily work.
- **Mid-level managers** delegate real authority, give actionable feedback, and stage stretch roles.
- **Executives** build systems and culture so development is expected, supported, and celebrated.

Development is not a perk; it's the work. This investment requires a shift in mindset. Leaders must see themselves not merely as decision-makers or problem-solvers but as developers of people.

Adopt a developer's mindset:
- *Who on my team needs encouragement to step forward?*
- *What opportunities can I create for others to lead?*
- *How can I model growth by sharing my own lessons learned?*

The returns are exponential. A leader who develops one person equips that person to lead others, creating a ripple effect that multiplies influence far beyond what the original leader could achieve alone. This is how leadership becomes legacy—through lives changed, confidence built, and leaders born.

Holistic leaders understand that people are not just resources; they are the enduring mission. By investing in others with consistency and care, leaders create something that outlasts their tenure: a community of people who believe in themselves, take ownership of their growth, and carry forward the vision.

Coaching and Mentorship in Context

Both coaching and mentorship have long histories, stretching back to some of the earliest human communities. Ancient apprenticeships paired young learners with masters who not only taught technical skills but also passed down wisdom, values, and a way of life.

A philosopher did not just teach logic; he modeled a way of seeing the world. These traditions remind us that leadership development has always been about more than productivity—it is about shaping people.

In more recent times, coaching emerged as a distinct discipline within leadership, education, and professional development. Once used primarily in athletics, coaching principles were adapted to the workplace to enhance performance, refine skills, and accelerate growth. Coaching today is a structured practice: it is time-bound, goal-driven, and centered on asking the right questions that unlock an individual's ability to solve problems and act with confidence.

Mentorship, in contrast, has retained its relational, long-term nature. While coaching may focus on today's tasks and skills, mentorship looks toward tomorrow's identity and vision. Mentorship is less about immediate performance and more about shaping the kind of leader someone is becoming. It involves wisdom-sharing, encouragement, accountability, and the gift of perspective that only comes from experience. These traditions point to two complementary practices modern leaders must master.

The Distinctions Matter:
- **Coaching** focuses on short-term performance. It is structured, practical, and often tied to measurable outcomes. Coaches ask questions such as: *"What is your goal? What challenges are you facing? What options do you see?"*
- **Mentorship** focuses on long-term development. It is relational, reflective, and identity-shaping. Mentors ask questions such as: *"What kind of leader do you want to become? What lessons are you drawing from this season? How will you carry your values into the future?"*

Why Leaders Need Both:
- Coaching ensures immediate effectiveness—helping people sharpen skills, increase confidence, and solve real-time problems.
- Mentorship ensures enduring growth—nurturing perspective, resilience, and vision that outlasts any single role or task.

The most effective leaders know how to move fluidly between these roles. Sometimes a team member needs targeted coaching to prepare for a presentation or to navigate a new system.

Other times, that same person needs mentorship—a safe space to wrestle with doubts about identity, career direction, or leadership purpose. Lead the moment with coaching; lead the horizon with mentorship.

When leaders combine coaching and mentorship, they don't just help people *do more*—they help people *become more*. They address both immediate potential and future possibilities, building teams that are not only effective in the moment but also prepared to carry the legacy of leadership forward. Frameworks make the practice repeatable.

Frameworks for Coaching and Mentorship

Coaching and mentorship are not abstract ideals; they are most powerful when grounded in proven frameworks that guide practice. These models give leaders practical tools to structure conversations, set expectations, and sustain growth. While frameworks are not meant to replace authenticity or intuition, they provide scaffolding so that development is intentional rather than accidental.

The GROW Model for Coaching

The GROW model—Goal, Reality, Options, Way Forward—is one of the most widely used and practical frameworks for coaching because it empowers rather than instructs. Instead of telling people what to do, leaders guide them through self-discovery and ownership of solutions.

1. **Goal** – Clarify the desired outcome.
    - *"What outcome matters most, specifically??"*
    - Goals should be specific, motivating, and within the person's control. For a frontline employee, this might mean improving time management; for an executive, it might mean shaping strategic priorities for a division.
2. **Reality** – Explore the current situation honestly.
    - *"What's true right now—evidence, constraints, assets?"*
    - This stage requires careful listening. Leaders help individuals see blind spots, assess strengths, and confront barriers.

3. **Options** – Open the conversation to possibilities.
   - *"List 3–5 ways forward—what are alternatives?*
   - The purpose here is creativity. Leaders encourage brainstorming without judgment. Even unconventional ideas can spark innovative solutions.
4. **Way Forward** – Commit to specific action.
   - *"What will you do by when, how will we follow up, and what support do you need?"*
   - This step ensures accountability. The person leaves the conversation with clarity, commitment, and next steps.

Close GROW with a timestamped commitment and a scheduled check-in. The GROW model is effective because it shifts ownership from leader to learner. It communicates trust and fosters independence—a hallmark of holistic leadership.

Developmental Mentoring

While coaching often focuses on immediate performance, **developmental mentoring** emphasizes long-term growth—shaping identity, wisdom, and purpose. A developmental mentor is less concerned with today's task and more concerned with tomorrow's leader.

Developmental mentoring often involves:
- Asking big-picture questions: *"What kind of leader do you want to be remembered as?"*
- Sharing personal stories that reveal lessons learned, both successes and failures.
- Encouraging reflection about values, vision, and legacy.

Offer perspective, not prescriptions. This form of mentoring is deeply relational. It is built on trust, vulnerability, and authenticity. It requires patience, because character formation is slow work. The rewards, however, are lasting. Leaders who engage in developmental mentoring do not just leave behind successors; they leave behind stewards of values and vision who carry culture forward long after structures change.

Situational Coaching

Not every follower needs the same kind of coaching. **Situational coaching**, drawn from the Situational Leadership model, emphasizes adapting your approach based on the person's skill, confidence, and readiness in a given area.

Four broad approaches emerge:
1. **Directing** – High direction, low support. Ideal for new or inexperienced team members who need step-by-step guidance.
    - Example: A new hire learning how to use critical software.
2. **Coaching** – High direction, high support. Beneficial for individuals who are eager but not yet fully competent.
    - Example: A staff member who has enthusiasm for leading a meeting but needs help structuring it.
3. **Supporting** – Low direction, high support. Appropriate for capable individuals who lack confidence or need encouragement.
    - Example: A seasoned employee taking on a stretch assignment.
4. **Delegating** – Low direction, low support. Effective when individuals are both competent and confident.
    - Example: A high-performing manager leading a project independently.

Select the mode by asking: skill level high/low? confidence high/low? Situational coaching communicates respect by meeting people where they are rather than treating everyone the same. It accelerates growth by providing precisely what is needed—no more, no less.

Reverse Mentorship

Reverse mentorship flips the traditional hierarchy. Here, younger or less experienced employees mentor senior leaders. This practice has become increasingly vital in times of rapid technological and cultural change.

For example, a Gen Z employee might mentor an executive on emerging digital platforms, fresh approaches to inclusion, or shifting workforce expectations. The executive, in turn, models humility by becoming a learner.

Reverse mentorship benefits both sides:
- Senior leaders gain new perspectives and avoid blind spots.
- Junior employees feel valued and empowered, knowing their insights matter.

Agree on two-way goals: what the executive will learn; what the mentor will practice (facilitation, influence, upward feedback). Leaders remembered for embracing reverse mentorship are known for curiosity, openness, and adaptability. They create cultures where growth is mutual and ego does not block innovation.

Peer Coaching Circles

Peer coaching circles bring together small groups of leaders or colleagues to coach one another. Unlike traditional coaching, which is one-directional, these circles are reciprocal—everyone is both coach and learner.

Structure: 60 minutes / 3 people / 20 minutes each: 2 minutes context, 12 minutes questions only, 4 minutes reflections, 2 minutes commitments.

A typical peer coaching circle works like this:
- One member presents a challenge or goal.
- Others listen actively, ask clarifying questions, and share observations.
- The group helps the presenter identify insights and action steps.

Over time, circles build trust, accountability, and collective wisdom. They are especially valuable for middle managers and executives who may not have many safe spaces to process challenges.

Peer circles also normalize vulnerability. When leaders admit challenges to their peers, they model authenticity and create environments where learning is collective. Organizations that embed peer coaching circles multiply wisdom across networks, not just within individual relationships.

Why These Frameworks Matter
Each framework addresses a different dimension of development:
- **GROW** – Structures immediate skill-building.
- **Developmental Mentoring** – Shapes identity and long-term growth.
- **Situational Coaching** – Adapts support based on readiness.
- **Reverse Mentorship** – Brings fresh perspectives and mutual learning.
- **Peer Coaching Circles** – Build collective wisdom and accountability.

When leaders employ these frameworks consistently, they do more than develop individuals—they build ecosystems of growth. And ecosystems, unlike individual programs, sustain themselves long after one leader has moved on.

Coaching as a Leadership Discipline
Coaching is not an optional add-on to leadership; it is a discipline—a consistent practice that shapes how leaders interact with their people. At its core, coaching is about drawing out potential rather than directing behavior. It is a way of leading that equips people to think critically, act independently, and grow beyond their current capacities.

Too often, leaders confuse coaching with managing. Management tends to focus on tasks, deadlines, and compliance. Coaching, by contrast, focuses on development, growth, and ownership. The manager asks, *"What needs to get done?"* The coach asks, *"Who are you becoming in the process of doing it?"* Both are important, but only coaching ensures that results are paired with growth.

Principles of Coaching as a Discipline:
1. **Ask Before Advising** – Instead of rushing in with solutions, effective coaches begin with questions. This draws out the other person's thinking and builds ownership of the solution.
2. **Focus on Strengths** – Coaching is not about fixing deficiencies but amplifying what someone already does well. People grow faster when their strengths are leveraged.
3. **Stay Present** – True coaching requires undivided attention. Leaders must set aside distractions, listen deeply, and create space where people feel heard.
4. **Challenge and Support** – Coaching is not passive encouragement. It is the art of balancing encouragement with stretch—helping people move beyond what is comfortable without feeling abandoned.
5. **End with Action** – Every coaching interaction should lead to clarity: *What will you do next? How will you practice this? What support do you need?*

When a team member was struggling with confidence in client conversations, I resisted the urge to give them a script. Instead, I asked them to reflect on times they had communicated successfully in the past. As they recalled their strengths, we identified specific techniques they could apply. Then I challenged them to practice those techniques in the next call while I observed. Afterward, we reflected together. That cycle of questioning, encouraging, and stretching transformed their performance more than any scripted advice could have.

Why Coaching as a Discipline Matters:
- It builds *ownership*: people commit to solutions they help create.
- It creates *independence*: team members learn to think and act without waiting for instructions.
- It strengthens *trust*: coaching communicates belief in a person's potential.
- It multiplies *capacity*: instead of one leader carrying the burden, the entire team develops problem-solving skills.

For Leaders at All Levels:
- **Supervisors** can coach team members to build confidence in day-to-day tasks.
- **Managers** can coach rising leaders to prepare them for bigger responsibilities.
- **Executives** can coach senior leaders to sharpen judgment and align decisions with values.

When practiced consistently, coaching shifts culture. People stop seeing their leader as the only source of answers and begin to see themselves as capable problem-solvers. Over time, coaching transforms a team from a group that depends on the leader to a community that multiplies leadership at every level.

Mentorship as a Leadership Discipline

If coaching is about unlocking immediate potential, mentorship is about shaping long-term growth. Mentorship is not a one-time conversation but a sustained relationship that helps people wrestle with questions of identity, purpose, and legacy. Where coaching often answers *"What should I do now?"*, mentorship asks *"Who am I becoming?"*

Unlike formal performance reviews or quick feedback loops, mentorship is a slower, more relational discipline. It requires consistency, presence, and trust. Mentorship is not about producing quick results; it is about forming leaders who carry values and vision forward long after the mentor has stepped away.

Principles of Mentorship as a Discipline:
1. **Be Consistent** – Show up regularly. Even brief check-ins build trust over time. Sporadic attention communicates that development is optional.
2. **Share Your Story** – Mentees learn not only from your advice but from your journey. Sharing your failures, lessons, and turning points gives them the perspective they can't get from a textbook.
3. **Guide, Don't Control** – Mentors offer perspective, not prescriptions. The goal is not to create copies of yourself but to help others discern their own leadership path.

4. **Model Vulnerability** – Effective mentors are honest about their weaknesses and mistakes. This gives permission for mentees to be authentic in their struggles.
5. **Celebrate Progress** – Growth is rarely linear. Mentors notice and affirm even small steps, building confidence and reinforcing resilience.

Why Mentorship as a Discipline Matters:
- It shapes *character* as well as competence.
- It builds *confidence* in emerging leaders who may not yet see their potential.
- It creates *continuity*—passing down values and vision that sustain culture.
- It multiplies *legacy*—leaders develop not only successors but stewards of the mission.

For Leaders at All Levels:
- **Supervisors** mentor by modeling integrity, resilience, and work ethic in daily interactions.
- **Managers** mentor by guiding team members into leadership opportunities and sharing lessons learned from their own journey.
- **Executives** mentor by shaping vision, culture, and legacy for the next generation of organizational leaders.

Mentorship, like coaching, requires discipline. It demands intentionality to prioritize people development amid urgent tasks. But leaders who embrace mentorship as a way of life extend their influence far beyond their tenure. They are remembered not only for what they built but for who they believed in.

Holistic leaders understand this truth: legacies are not carried forward by projects or programs but by people. Mentorship is the discipline of ensuring that those people are prepared to lead with confidence, character, and clarity for years to come.

Coaching and Mentorship Across Leadership Levels

A front-line supervisor, a mid-level manager, and a senior executive all have opportunities to coach and mentor—but the focus shifts depending on where they stand. Think scope: *frontline = moments, middle = pathways, senior = pipelines*.

For Frontline Leaders: Coaching and mentorship often happen in real time, in the rhythm of daily work. A frontline leader may coach a team member on handling a difficult customer interaction or mentor them by sharing how to navigate the early stages of their career. The impact is immediate and practical: people feel supported where they are, and they see their leader as a guide, not just a task manager.

For Middle Managers: The role shifts to developing people not only for performance but also for progression. Middle managers are uniquely positioned to spot potential in their teams and prepare them for broader responsibilities. They must balance short-term coaching for skill with long-term mentorship that nurtures vision. Their influence is multiplied because they shape both individuals and entire departments.

For Senior Executives: At the highest levels, coaching and mentorship take on a strategic dimension. Executives coach their leaders to sharpen decision-making, expand perspective, and stay aligned with organizational vision. They mentor by sharing lessons about identity, resilience, and legacy—preparing the next generation to carry forward not just strategies but values.

Across all levels, the principle remains constant: leaders grow leaders. The scope may differ, but the responsibility is the same. Leaders who embed coaching and mentorship into their daily practice ensure that development does not depend on a single program or initiative; it becomes part of the culture.

Practical Mentorship Habits

1. **Be consistent.** Meet regularly — monthly or quarterly at a minimum.
2. **Share your story.** People learn as much from your journey as from your advice.
3. **Guide, don't control.** Offer perspective but let them make decisions.
4. **Model vulnerability.** Share lessons learned from your own mistakes and growth.
5. **Make measurable.** Agree on 1–2 outcome markers per quarter (e.g., led X meeting, shipped Y proposal).
6. **Celebrate progress.** Mark milestones of growth, however small.

Scaling Development in Groups

Not all development happens one-on-one. Teams and cohorts can also benefit from coaching and mentorship practices.

In one workgroup, I set aside time at the end of a project for collective reflection. I asked: *"What have we learned about ourselves in this process?"* The answers were candid and revealing. People discovered strengths they hadn't named before and acknowledged areas for growth. That single practice of group reflection multiplied learning across the team.

Practical Group Practices

Teams and cohorts can also grow together when leaders embed coaching and mentorship practices into group settings. These shared approaches multiply learning, build trust, and create cultures where development is part of the team's DNA.

Structured Reflection Sessions: Invite the team to pause and reflect at the end of a project, quarter, or major initiative. Ask three simple but powerful questions: *What worked? What didn't? What did we learn?* This shifts the focus from just results to growth. Reflection sessions help normalize learning from both successes and failures. They also democratize insight—junior team members may surface observations that senior leaders missed. Over time, these sessions reinforce a growth mindset where every experience becomes an opportunity for collective learning.

Rotating Facilitation: Allowing different team members to facilitate meetings distributes leadership and builds confidence. When a new voice leads, they gain valuable practice in communication, organization, and influence. For frontline teams, rotating facilitation may mean leading a five-minute safety briefing. For senior leadership groups, it may mean steering a complex strategic discussion. Either way, rotating facilitation signals that leadership is shared, not centralized, and that everyone has the capacity to influence the team.

Peer Mentorship: Pair team members intentionally so they can support one another's growth. Peer mentorship removes hierarchy and creates safe spaces for honest dialogue. For example, a newer employee might mentor a colleague in digital tools, while receiving mentorship in return about organizational culture. Managers can set up peer mentorship circles where pairs or trios check in monthly on goals and challenges. This practice normalizes mutual learning and builds a culture where everyone both gives and receives support.

Group Coaching Questions: Start team meetings with a coaching-style question to spark reflection and creativity. Instead of diving straight into tasks, ask prompts such as:
- *"What opportunity do we see in this challenge?"*
- *"What's one strength we can lean on as a team right now?"*
- *"What lesson from last week should guide us this week?"* These questions shift focus from problems to possibilities and remind the team that development is ongoing. They also give space for diverse voices to contribute, often surfacing insights that shape strategy or morale in unexpected ways.

Building a Coaching and Mentorship Culture

The best leaders do not keep coaching and mentorship to themselves; they create cultures where development is expected, encouraged, and supported across the organization. In such cultures, growth is not dependent on a single leader's effort but becomes part of the fabric of the team's identity. Everyone—from new employees to senior executives—knows that developing others is part of what it means to lead.

A coaching and mentorship culture sends a powerful message: *"We believe in people enough to invest in them, and we expect every leader to do the same."* When this becomes the norm, organizations gain not only higher performance but deeper loyalty, greater resilience, and stronger succession pipelines.

Practices for Building Culture
1. **Normalize Feedback:** Feedback should be a rhythm, not a rare event. In a strong culture, conversations about growth happen naturally—in hallways, during meetings, and in project debriefs. Leaders model this by both giving and receiving feedback openly, demonstrating that it is not criticism but a gift that drives development. Model by asking, *"What's one way I could have led that better?"*
2. **Match Mentors and Mentees Intentionally:** Pair people based on growth needs, not convenience. A new manager might be paired with a senior leader known for coaching skills, while a high-potential employee might be paired with someone who has navigated similar challenges. Intentional pairing ensures that mentorship feels purposeful rather than perfunctory.
3. **Celebrate Development:** Recognize leaders who invest in others. Too often, organizations reward only visible achievements like revenue or project completion. By also celebrating those who coach and mentor, leaders communicate that developing people is as valuable as delivering results. This can take the form of awards, shout-outs in meetings, or storytelling that highlights how someone's investment shaped another's growth.
4. **Provide Training:** Not all leaders naturally know how to coach or mentor. Provide practical training that equips them with frameworks, tools, and confidence to invest in others effectively. Workshops, role-playing, or even peer-learning groups can help emerging leaders build these critical skills.
5. **Protect Time:** Coaching and mentorship must be scheduled as non-negotiables, not squeezed in "when time allows." Leaders should have dedicated space for one-on-one development conversations, group reflection sessions, or mentoring check-ins. Block recurring 30–45 minutes as appropriate, and decline lower-priority items to protect it. When development is on the calendar, it communicates that people matter as much as projects. If it isn't on the calendar, it isn't in the culture.

Why Culture Matters

When coaching and mentorship are embedded into culture, leadership multiplies. Growth no longer depends on a single leader but becomes a shared responsibility. A frontline supervisor sees it as normal to coach team members in daily interactions. A middle manager views mentorship as part of their job, not an extra. An executive ensures systems, policies, and recognition structures reinforce development at scale.

The long-term result is a community of leaders who know how to invest in others because they have been invested in themselves. Over time, this creates a legacy of leadership that continues to grow, generation after generation.

Practical Tools
Coaching Questions to Use Now
- What's your biggest priority right now?
- What feels most challenging, and why?
- What options have you considered?
- What's one step you could take this week?
- What did you learn from your last project?

Mentorship Rhythms
- Start with life, then work.
- Meet monthly or quarterly.
- Begin with life and values before moving to work.
- Share a resource — an article, book, or story that shaped you.
- Ask: *"What's one thing you'd like to grow in this year?"*

Daily Integration
- Start team meetings with a coaching-style question.
- End projects with a mentorship-style reflection.
- Ask each leader on your team to invest intentionally in one person.
- Ask each leader to name one person they are actively developing—by name.

From Theory to Practice

Coaching and mentorship are daily skills. Ten focused minutes, repeated, beat a quarterly seminar. Like any discipline, they grow stronger with use. Leaders who consistently apply coaching and mentorship create environments where people are not only managed but also developed, not only directed but also believed in.

Translating theory into practice requires leaders to shift their mindset from *occasional development* to *ongoing investment*. Development does not have to be formal or lengthy—sometimes the most powerful growth happens in a ten-minute conversation, a thoughtful question, or a word of encouragement at the right time. What matters is consistency.

Five Daily Practices

1. **Prepare with Intentionality:** Before every developmental conversation, pause to clarify your role. Does this moment call for **coaching**, where the focus is short-term skills and problem-solving, or for **mentorship**, where the focus is long-term identity and growth? Leaders who prepare intentionally avoid the mistake of giving advice when they should be listening, or rushing to solve when they should be guiding reflection.
2. **Listen More Than You Speak:** Effective coaching and mentorship are grounded in presence. Aim for 70% listening and 30% speaking. Active listening communicates respect and often reveals underlying fears, strengths, or blind spots that surface only when people feel truly heard. Leaders who listen deeply earn the credibility to influence meaningfully.
3. **Ask Powerful Questions:** Growth rarely comes from telling people what to do; it comes from asking questions that spark reflection. Ask, *"What outcome do you want?"* and *"What's one step this week?"* Powerful questions unlock ownership and self-discovery, which is far more sustainable than dependency on the leader.

4. **Document Growth:** Encourage people to write down their goals, insights, and progress. Documentation turns fleeting conversations into tangible milestones. This can be as simple as keeping a personal growth journal, tracking achievements in one-on-ones, or maintaining a mentorship log. Capture actions in a shared note: *owner/date/proof.* Recording growth helps individuals see how far they've come, which fuels motivation and resilience.
5. **Close with Encouragement:** Every coaching or mentorship interaction should end with affirmation. This doesn't mean avoiding hard truths—it means pairing challenge with belief. A leader might say: *"I know this will stretch you, but I believe you're ready,"* or *"This didn't go perfectly, but I see your progress and your persistence."* Encouragement reinforces that growth is not about perfection but about possibility. People grow when they know their leader sees potential in them, even when they don't yet see it themselves.

Practice creates culture; culture compounds. I make it a habit to end every developmental conversation with affirmation. It doesn't erase the challenge, but it reframes it. When someone leaves a conversation knowing their leader believes in them, they face the challenge with greater confidence. Over time, this simple habit changes culture: people begin to believe not just in their leader, but in themselves.

Why Practice Matters

Without practice, coaching and mentorship remain good intentions. With practice, they become transformational habits. For frontline supervisors, this may look like turning routine check-ins into growth conversations. For mid-level managers, it may mean creating rhythms of mentorship across the department. For executives, it means modeling development publicly so the entire organization sees that investing in people is a non-negotiable priority.

When leaders bring coaching and mentorship from theory into daily practice, they multiply their influence. They build not only competent teams but also confident leaders. They ensure that legacy is not measured only in what they accomplished but in who they developed along the way.

Pitfalls & Best Practices

Pitfall 1: Treating Coaching as Giving Answers
- Example: Jumping in with solutions instead of guiding reflection.
- Best Practice: Ask open-ended questions that unlock ownership.

Pitfall 2: Limiting Mentorship to Formal Programs
- Example: Waiting for an "official" mentoring structure before investing in others.
- Best Practice: Recognize informal moments as powerful mentoring opportunities.

Pitfall 3: Investing Only in High Performers
- Example: Giving all attention to rising stars while neglecting quiet contributors.
- Best Practice: Look for hidden potential in everyone.

Pitfall 4: Mentoring Without Modeling
- Example: Offering advice but living inconsistently.
- Best Practice: Let mentees see your values in action.

Pitfall 5: Neglecting Succession Thinking
- Example: Developing people without preparing them to lead others.
- Best Practice: Mentor with multiplication in mind — leaders who make leaders.

Pitfall 6: Vague Next Steps
- Best Practice: End every conversation with owner + action + date + check-in.

Reflective Questions
1. Do you naturally lean more toward coaching or mentorship?
2. Who are you currently coaching, and what is their next growth step?
3. Who are you mentoring for long-term leadership development?
4. How do you ensure developmental conversations end with clarity and encouragement?
5. What systems could you create to scale coaching and mentorship across your team?

Journaling Prompts
- Write about a time you helped someone discover confidence they didn't know they had.
- Reflect on how mentorship has shaped your own journey.
- Journal about the last coaching question you asked. How did it change the conversation?
- Record the name of a person you could begin mentoring this year.

90-Day Coaching and Mentorship Growth Plan

Month 1 – Begin the Rhythm
- Identify one person to coach and one to mentor.
- Schedule one coaching session and one mentorship meeting.

Month 2 – Deepen the Practice
- Use GROW in two conversations; capture G, R, O, W in notes.
- Establish a monthly rhythm with your mentee, focusing on both career and character.

Month 3 – Multiply the Impact
- Facilitate one group reflection session with your team.
- Facilitate one peer coaching conversation for your team.
- Share one story of mentorship impact to inspire others to invest.

By the end of 90 days, you will not only strengthen your own coaching and mentorship skills but also set in motion a culture where growth and leadership development are daily expectations, not occasional events. Coaching and mentorship ensure that leadership does not end with you. When you develop others, you multiply influence, extend vision, and build a legacy of leaders who will carry the work forward with integrity and courage.

Multiplying leaders requires protecting the trust that multiplies them—ethics is not a brake; it's the steering wheel. Next, we turn to ethical decision-making.

7 ETHICAL DECISION-MAKING

Ethics is not optional—it is the foundation of leadership. Skills earn influence, vision attracts followers, but without moral courage, trust erodes, and legacy is lost. Leadership is tested when doing right costs something. Ethical leaders show clarity of values and courage under pressure, while others look for shortcuts. Those moments define not only outcomes but also reputation and legacy.

Choosing Values When It Matters Most

I once sat in a meeting where a decision could have saved time and resources if we had compromised on a standard. All eyes turned to me, waiting for approval. I paused, knowing the easier choice would move things forward quickly. Instead, I said, *"This might cost us more now, but if it isn't consistent with our values, it isn't the right path."*

The room grew quiet, but the tone was set. That moment reminded me that ethical leadership is rarely about convenience. It is about courage—courage to stand for what is right, even when the pressure is high, the room is silent, or the cost is real.

Why Ethics Is a Strategic Imperative

Without ethics, vision loses credibility, strategy loses integrity, and results lose meaning. Ethics is not theory—it is strategy. Ethics in leadership is not abstract philosophy; it is a daily necessity. Without it, vision loses credibility, strategy loses integrity, and results lose meaning. The finest goals and most sophisticated plans collapse if they are not anchored in trust. Ethical leadership is not only about doing what is right—it is about ensuring that people believe in the process, the outcomes, and the leaders guiding them.

Leaders who embody ethics earn trust, inspire loyalty, and shape cultures that endure. Trust is the ultimate currency of leadership. Without it, even the most talented leader cannot mobilize people effectively. With it, leaders can rally teams through seasons of uncertainty, resistance, and change. Loyalty born from trust produces resilience, creativity, and long-term commitment—qualities that no incentive program or short-term strategy can replicate.

Every leader, regardless of level, faces moments where values and expedience collide:

- A **supervisor** deciding whether to cover for a mistake or own it honestly.
- A **manager** choosing between fairness to the team and pressure to reward only top performers.
- An **executive** weighing whether to sacrifice long-term trust for short-term financial gain.

In each case, the easier path may bring immediate relief, but only the ethical path sustains trust and builds a legacy.

Holistic leaders understand this: ethics is not an added layer to leadership but its very core. It shapes how decisions are made, how people are treated, and how legacies are written. Leadership without ethics may shine brightly for a season, but it cannot endure.

- Leaders who compromised ethics for expedience may have won temporary victories, but their downfalls were permanent. Their names are remembered, but not admired.
- Leaders who held fast to values, even when costly, left legacies that continue to inspire. Their influence outlasted their tenure because their integrity outlived their accomplishments.

For holistic leaders, ethics is not a "nice-to-have" or a secondary concern. It is the compass by which every decision must be guided. Just as a ship cannot safely sail without a true north, leaders cannot navigate complexity without values. Strategy without ethics is aimless; it may reach a destination, but it will not be one worth celebrating.

Why Ethics Must Be Strategic:
1. **It Safeguards Reputation.** In an age of instant transparency, unethical choices are exposed faster than ever. Ethics protects leaders and organizations from self-inflicted damage.
2. **It Guides Complex Decisions.** When faced with competing priorities, ethical principles provide clarity that numbers alone cannot. They help leaders choose not just what is effective, but what is right.
3. **It Sustains Culture.** Cultures are shaped by what leaders reward, tolerate, and ignore. An ethical leader ensures that culture reinforces dignity, fairness, and trust.
4. **It Creates Long-Term Value.** Ethical decisions may cost more in the short term but pay dividends in loyalty, resilience, and legacy. Integrity compounds like interest over time.

For Leaders at All Levels:
- A **supervisor** who refuses to misreport hours models integrity to their team.
- A **manager** who protects fairness in promotions builds trust across departments.
- An **executive** who prioritizes ethical practices over short-term profit shapes culture for the entire organization.

Holistic leaders understand that strategy and ethics are inseparable. A strategic plan without ethical grounding is fragile, but a values-driven strategy inspires confidence, unites people, and endures beyond the leader. Ethics is not a constraint on strategy—it is the force that gives it credibility, resilience, and meaning.

The Evolution of Ethical Thought in Leadership
Three traditions shape modern leadership ethics: virtue, duty, and consequences.

1. **Virtue Ethics** – Rooted in Aristotle and Aquinas, this view emphasizes character. Leaders become ethical by cultivating virtues like courage, honesty, justice, and temperance. Leadership flows out of who you are.
2. **Deontological Ethics (Duty-Based)** – Associated with Immanuel Kant, this approach focuses on principles. Some actions are right or wrong regardless of outcomes. Leaders must uphold duties like honesty, fairness, and respect for human dignity.
3. **Consequentialism (Outcome-Based)** – This perspective emphasizes results. The ethical choice is the one that creates the greatest good for the greatest number. Leaders weigh impact and seek outcomes that serve collective well-being.

No single framework is enough on its own. Holistic leaders draw from all three: anchoring their character in virtue, their choices in principle (duty), and their strategies in outcomes (consequences) that serve the greater good. Together, they provide a comprehensive framework for ethical decision-making.

Ethics in Everyday Leadership

When people think of ethics in leadership, they often imagine high-profile dilemmas—corporate scandals, political decisions, or crises in the public eye. Yet the accurate measure of ethical leadership is not found only in dramatic moments. It is revealed in ordinary, everyday choices—how leaders assign work, share credit, and handle truth.

Every leader, at every level, faces small but significant tests of integrity. A frontline supervisor may choose whether to speak honestly about scheduling challenges or "make it work" by overburdening one employee. A manager may decide whether to share credit with the team or present ideas as their own. An executive may weigh whether to approve a shortcut that improves quarterly numbers but undermines long-term trust.

These everyday moments matter because they send signals that shape culture. When a leader overlooks disrespectful behavior in a meeting, the team learns that incivility is tolerated. When a leader consistently recognizes effort, the team learns that growth is valued as much as results. Every choice either reinforces or erodes the values the leader claims to uphold.

Examples of Everyday Ethical Leadership:
- **Transparency in Communication** – Sharing not only the good news but also the complex realities, so people know they can trust what you say.
- **Fairness in Opportunity** – Distributing assignments in equitable ways, not based on favoritism.
- **Respect in Meetings** – Ensuring every voice is heard and that ideas are not dismissed because of hierarchy or personality.
- **Integrity in Credit** – Publicly acknowledging contributions rather than allowing silence to imply ideas or successes originated from you alone.

What may feel like "small decisions" in the moment often leave the deepest impressions. Years later, people may not remember the quarterly results. Still, they will remember whether their leader was honest in difficult conversations, whether their contributions were valued, and whether their dignity was preserved.

Holistic leaders understand this: ethics is not a spotlight event but a daily practice. It is woven into conversations, decisions, and relationships. Leaders who take ethics seriously in small moments find themselves ready when larger tests come. Those who compromise in everyday life often find themselves unprepared when the stakes are high.

The Cost of Ethical Leadership
Ethical leadership is inspiring to talk about, but costly to live out. Doing the right thing often comes with a price—financial, relational, or reputational. Leaders who anchor themselves in values rather than convenience must be prepared to face resistance, misunderstanding, and sometimes loss.

The costs can include:
- **Short-Term Sacrifice** – Choosing the ethical path may slow progress or increase expenses. Refusing to cut corners might mean missing deadlines or investing more resources.
- **Relational Strain** – Ethical choices can strain relationships with peers, superiors, or stakeholders who prefer expedience. A leader who refuses to compromise may be labeled "difficult" or "idealistic."
- **Personal Pressure** – Standing firm in ethical decisions often brings isolation, especially when others take the easier road. Moral courage requires resilience when applause is absent.

I once chose to communicate the reality of performance numbers honestly, even though "polishing" the results would have made us look better to external partners. Tension rose at first, but over time, honesty built trust that spin never could. Integrity carried a short-term cost but yielded long-term credibility.

History confirms this pattern. Leaders who sacrificed ethics for quick wins often secured temporary victories but endured permanent downfalls. By contrast, leaders who accepted the cost of doing right—whether financial loss, slowed progress, or personal criticism—left legacies of trust that outlasted opposition.

The Paradox of Ethical Leadership:
- The ethical path often costs more in the moment but creates returns over time.
- The unethical path often rewards quickly but destroys credibility in the long run.

Holistic leaders embrace this paradox. They understand that every principled decision is an investment in trust, credibility, and culture. While the cost may feel heavy in the present, the dividends compound into a legacy.

In the end, the question is not whether ethical leadership is costly—it is whether leaders are willing to pay the price today to leave behind a legacy tomorrow.

The Role of Accountability in Ethical Leadership

Ethical leadership does not thrive in isolation. Even the most principled leaders need structures, relationships, and practices that keep them grounded. Accountability is the safeguard that ensures values are not just spoken but lived. Without it, blind spots expand, rationalizations creep in, and pressure can slowly erode conviction.

Accountability takes different forms—peer, structural, and personal—and each plays a vital role in sustaining ethical leadership.

1. Peer Accountability

Leaders need trusted peers who can speak truth without fear of retribution. These are colleagues, mentors, or advisors who are willing to ask hard questions:

- *"Are you being consistent with your values?"*
- *"What pressures are shaping this decision?"*
- *"How might this affect people you haven't considered?"*

Peer accountability provides perspective and reminds leaders that they are not immune to bias. When leaders surround themselves with people who only affirm them, they risk drifting into self-deception. Honest peers, by contrast, act as mirrors—reflecting reality when leaders are tempted to ignore it.

2. Structural Accountability

Organizations must also embed accountability into systems. Policies, audits, transparent reporting, and oversight boards are not bureaucratic burdens; they are safeguards against ethical drift.

- Clear conflict-of-interest policies prevent hidden compromises.
- Transparent financial systems protect against misuse of resources.
- Oversight committees provide checks and balances on major decisions.

Leaders who embrace these structures signal confidence that their choices can withstand scrutiny. Rather than resisting accountability systems, ethical leaders welcome them as tools to protect integrity and trust.

3. Personal Accountability

Finally, leaders must hold themselves accountable through intentional practices of reflection and discipline. This might include:

- **Journaling** key decisions and the values that guided them.
- **Daily reflection** on moments of tension: *"Did I choose integrity today, or did I take the easier path?"*
- **Mentorship relationships** where leaders share their struggles honestly.

Personal accountability ensures that leaders are not only answerable to others but also honest with themselves. Over time, these practices sharpen conscience and prevent compromise from becoming normalized.

Example in Practice:
I once worked with an executive who created a personal practice of reviewing every major decision by asking, *"Would I be proud to explain this to my children?"* That simple filter, paired with a peer circle that challenged him regularly, kept his leadership anchored when pressure mounted. His willingness to submit to accountability systems, both personal and organizational, modeled humility and built lasting trust.

Why Accountability Matters
- It prevents ethical drift in moments of pressure.
- It provides leaders with perspectives they cannot see on their own.
- It strengthens cultures of integrity by showing that no one is above examination.

Holistic leaders recognize that accountability is not a sign of weakness but of wisdom. By welcoming it, they protect their integrity, inspire trust in their teams, and build organizations where ethical leadership is the norm rather than the exception. In the end, accountability is not about limitation—it is about freedom: the freedom to lead boldly, knowing your values are safeguarded by the structures and people around you.

Frameworks for Ethical Decision-Making

The Ethics Test: One of the most straightforward and practical tools for ethical decision-making is the ethics test. It asks two critical questions: *Would I be comfortable if this decision were public? Who benefits, and who bears the cost?* These questions cut through rationalization and force leaders to examine both transparency and fairness. A decision that can withstand the scrutiny of the front page of a newspaper—or the test of explaining it to your children—has integrity at its core. Asking who benefits and who pays prevents leaders from overlooking hidden consequences. Ethical leaders don't stop at what is legal; they pursue what is just. Over time, consistent use of this test builds reputations of trustworthiness that outlast any single decision.

The PLUS Model: The PLUS model (Policies, Legal, Universal values, and Self) provides a structured checklist for decision-making:
- **Policies:** Does this decision align with organizational rules and procedures?
- **Legal:** Is it consistent with laws and regulations?
- **Universal values:** Does it reflect fairness, honesty, and respect for all?
- **Self:** Does this decision align with my personal values and conscience?

This framework ensures leaders evaluate choices from multiple perspectives before acting. It closes loopholes where leaders might justify questionable decisions by appealing to one dimension (e.g., legality) while ignoring another (e.g., universal fairness). Leaders who apply PLUS demonstrate that ethics are multi-layered, not one-dimensional, and that alignment across all four areas is essential.

Values Alignment Filter: Every decision either reinforces or erodes the culture a leader claims to uphold. The values alignment filter asks: *Does this decision strengthen or weaken our stated values?* For example, if an organization's core value is collaboration but a decision rewards individual achievement at the expense of teamwork, the culture will shift toward competition. Leaders must recognize that values are not preserved by slogans on a wall but by the daily decisions leaders make and reward. By applying this filter, leaders ensure consistency between what they say and what they do—a consistency that shapes culture and builds legacy.

Stakeholder Mapping: Stakeholder mapping expands the ethical lens by asking: *Who will be affected by this decision, and how?* Leaders identify key groups—employees, customers, communities, shareholders, even future generations—and examine the equity of impact. Stakeholder mapping prevents tunnel vision, where leaders optimize for one group while unintentionally harming another. For example, cutting costs might benefit shareholders but devastate employees or communities. By weighing all stakeholders, leaders make choices that are not only profitable but sustainable. Leaders remembered for fairness are those who saw the whole picture and chose equity over expedience.

The Legacy Question: Perhaps the most profound ethical filter is also the simplest: *Will this decision matter ten years from now?* This question pulls leaders out of short-term pressure and into long-term perspective. It asks them to imagine their future selves—or their successors—looking back at the choice. Would they be proud? Would the organization be stronger? Would trust have been preserved? Leaders who live by this question refuse to trade enduring integrity for temporary advantage. They understand that every decision leaves ripples, some visible today, others only years later. The legacy-minded leader makes decisions that will still look wise when history reflects on them.

Moral Courage: The Missing Ingredient

Knowing what is right is never enough. The gap between conviction and action is bridged by courage—specifically, moral courage. While technical competence and strategic insight can position someone as a leader, it is moral courage that proves whether they truly are one.

Moral courage is the willingness to uphold values in the face of fear, pressure, or personal loss. It is choosing principle over popularity, truth over convenience, and integrity over expedience. Courage is not the absence of fear but the refusal to let fear dictate action. Leaders with moral courage acknowledge risks, anticipate opposition, and sometimes endure loss—yet they act anyway.

Why Moral Courage Matters:
- **It protects integrity.** Without courage, leaders know the right choice but fail to act on it.
- **It earns trust.** Teams respect leaders who take risks to uphold values, even when outcomes are uncertain.
- **It sets culture.** Every courageous decision raises the standard for what others believe is possible.

I have had moments where I knew my decision would not be well-received. The easier option would have been silence or compromise. But I chose to stand firm, even when it created tension in the room. The resistance was real in the moment, but over time, people came to trust that my decisions were anchored in principle, not convenience. That trust became the foundation of lasting influence.

The Barriers to Moral Courage:
- **Fear of Rejection:** Leaders fear alienating stakeholders, peers, or employees.
- **Fear of Loss:** Ethical choices may mean losing profit, position, or short-term success.
- **Fear of Isolation:** Taking a stand often feels lonely, especially if others prefer the easier path.

Practices That Strengthen Moral Courage:
1. **Clarify Core Values.** Leaders who know their non-negotiables are less likely to compromise under pressure.
2. **Rehearse Difficult Conversations.** Preparation reduces fear by making the hard choice familiar.
3. **Seek Allies.** Courage grows stronger when leaders surround themselves with others who share their commitment to integrity.
4. **Celebrate Acts of Courage.** Recognize and reward moments when people uphold values, even at a cost. This normalizes bravery across the culture.
5. **Reflect on Legacy.** Ask, *"How will this choice be remembered in ten years?"* A long-term perspective often outweighs short-term fear.

For Leaders at All Levels:
- A **supervisor** demonstrates moral courage when they hold a high performer accountable for misconduct.
- A **manager** shows courage when they tell upper leadership the truth about challenges rather than hiding problems.
- An **executive** models courage when they reject a profitable opportunity that conflicts with the organization's values.

Practices for Developing Moral Courage in Teams
1. **Model Vulnerability.** Admit when you struggle with tough decisions.
2. **Celebrate Ethical Choices.** Recognize when team members uphold values, even at a cost.
3. **Create Safe Channels.** Provide ways for people to raise ethical concerns without fear.
4. **Reinforce Identity.** Remind teams, *"This is who we are — our values guide us."*

Moral courage is the missing ingredient because it turns knowledge into action. Many leaders know the right thing to do, but only those who act—despite fear—become leaders worth following.

Holistic leaders understand this truth: legacies are not written by what we intended but by what we had the courage to do.

The Cost of Compromise

Every leader faces ethical crossroads. Rarely do these moments arrive with flashing warning lights. More often, they appear in the form of seemingly small decisions—approving a shortcut, overlooking a policy, withholding an uncomfortable truth, or rationalizing that "everyone does it." Each concession makes the next easier. Over time, small compromises accumulate, shaping culture, eroding credibility, and setting precedents that are difficult to reverse.

The danger of compromise lies in its subtlety. Few leaders set out intending to violate values in dramatic ways. Instead, culture erodes through incremental concessions. A leader who approves one shortcut finds it easier to approve another. A supervisor who ignores one breach of policy struggles to enforce it later. A manager who spins results once feels pressure to spin again. Before long, compromise is no longer the exception—it becomes the norm.

I once faced this temptation on a project where our performance numbers fell short of expectations. It would have been easy to "spin" the results, highlighting selective wins and downplaying the gaps. That narrative might have satisfied external partners in the short term, but it would have undermined the very trust our team depended on. Instead, I chose to present the reality honestly and paired it with a clear improvement plan. The conversation was harder in the moment, but it built trust that lasted far longer than any polished narrative could have.

Why Compromise Costs More Than It Saves:
1. **It Erodes Trust.** Once people suspect that a leader shades the truth or overlooks values, every future decision is questioned.
2. **It Weakens Culture.** What leaders tolerate becomes the team's standard. A single compromise signals that integrity is optional.
3. **It Damages Legacy.** Results achieved through compromise may be forgotten, but the breach of trust remains in memory.

For Leaders at All Levels:
- A **supervisor** who ignores inappropriate behavior sets a precedent that undermines team morale.
- A **manager** who avoids hard conversations erodes accountability in their department.
- An **executive** who compromises values for profit undermines culture across the organization.

Holistic leaders recognize that the easiest choice is not always the right choice. Compromise may relieve pressure in the short term, but integrity sustains influence in the long run. Honesty, even when costly, is always more sustainable than spin.

Redemption and Ethical Recovery

Even the best leaders stumble. Ethical failure—whether through poor judgment, unchecked pressure, or simple neglect—is part of the human condition. The actual test of leadership is not whether one avoids every misstep but how one responds when integrity is compromised.

Too often, leaders believe that an ethical lapse permanently disqualifies them from influence. In reality, failure does not have to end a leader's legacy if it is met with humility, accountability, and change. Redemption is possible—but only for those willing to face the truth.

The Difference Between Collapse and Recovery

- **Cover-Up**: When leaders hide, excuse, or minimize their failures, trust erodes further. Minor lapses spiral into larger scandals when leaders refuse to admit mistakes.
- **Confession**: When leaders acknowledge failure openly and accept responsibility, they create the possibility of restored trust. People are often more willing to forgive failure than deceit.

Cover-up erodes trust further. Confession opens the door to recovery.

The Path to Ethical Recovery

1. **Own It Quickly** – Acknowledge what happened without shifting blame. Transparency is the first step to regaining credibility.
2. **Apologize and Repair** – Seek forgiveness from those affected and take practical steps to repair harm. An apology without restitution is incomplete.
3. **Learn and Change** – Put structures in place to prevent repeat failures. This might mean creating new accountability systems, seeking mentorship, or adjusting decision-making processes.
4. **Model Vulnerability** – Share lessons learned so others can avoid the same mistakes. Ethical recovery can be a powerful teaching moment for the entire team.

Example in Practice:

I once worked alongside a leader who made a decision that unintentionally violated organizational policy. Instead of justifying it or hiding it, they immediately admitted the mistake, explained their reasoning, and worked with the team to correct the outcome. While some were frustrated in the short term, that act of humility deepened trust. The team knew this leader was not perfect—but they were honest. Over time, their influence actually grew because people saw them as authentic and accountable.

Why Redemption Matters
- It reminds teams that ethical leadership is not about perfection but about integrity in the aftermath of imperfection.
- It creates a culture where people feel safe to admit mistakes, rather than hiding them out of fear.
- It ensures that failure does not become final, but formative.

Holistic leaders understand that failure can be a classroom. When handled with humility, an ethical lapse can become a defining moment that strengthens both the leader and the culture. The scars of past mistakes, when carried with honesty, often become the very stories that inspire future generations to lead with greater courage.

In the end, legacy is not only shaped by the victories we achieve but also by the failures we redeem. Ethical recovery teaches that while compromise is costly, redemption—through humility, confession, and growth—is always possible.

Ethical Decision-Making Model

Ethical leadership demands more than good intentions; it requires a disciplined process for making decisions under pressure. In the complexity of leadership, where competing priorities and conflicting interests often collide, a structured model provides clarity and consistency. The following seven-step framework offers a practical roadmap for aligning choices with values, protecting trust, and sustaining integrity.

1. Define the Issue Clearly: Before making any decision, leaders must ask: *"What exactly is at stake?"* Ethical dilemmas often feel overwhelming because they are clouded by competing narratives or hidden assumptions. Clarity requires stripping away distractions to name the core tension.

2. Gather the Facts: Good ethics cannot be built on incomplete information. Leaders must distinguish between facts, assumptions, and rumors. Ask: *"What do we know? What do we not know?"* This step protects against hasty choices and ensures decisions rest on reality rather than perception.

3. Identify Stakeholders: Every decision affects people, often in ways leaders may not see at first glance. Identifying stakeholders broadens perspective and prevents tunnel vision. Ask: *"Who will be affected by this decision, and how?"*

4. Evaluate Options Against Values: Leaders must ask whether each option aligns with integrity, fairness, and justice. Does it reflect the organization's mission? Does it honor human dignity? Here, values serve as the filter, not just outcomes.

5. Test the Decision: Ethical clarity often comes through simple questions: *"Would I be comfortable if this were public? Would I want my family or my team to know I made this choice?"* If the decision cannot withstand transparency, it cannot claim integrity.

6. Decide and Act: Once the decision is made, leaders must act decisively and communicate it clearly. Ethical hesitation erodes trust as much as unethical action. By explaining the *why* behind the decision, leaders model both transparency and conviction.

7. Reflect and Learn: After the decision, leaders must ask: *"What did this reveal about our culture and values? Did our processes support or hinder ethical clarity?"* Reflection turns one decision into learning that strengthens future choices.

Frameworks don't remove tension, but they keep decisions aligned with values when pressure is highest.

Why Models and Tests Matter
- They prevent hasty compromises when pressure is high.
- They provide consistency across leaders and levels of the organization.
- They transform ethics from abstract ideals into actionable practices.

Holistic leaders do not rely on instincts alone. They embrace frameworks that guide them when pressure, fear, or complexity threatens clarity. By practicing disciplined ethical decision-making, leaders not only protect their integrity but also build cultures where values are trusted as the compass for every choice.

From Theory to Practice
Ethical leadership cannot remain in theory or lofty ideals. It must be lived out daily, not only in high-profile decisions but also in the small, unseen choices that reveal a leader's true priorities. Integrity is not built in one dramatic moment but in the quiet consistency of daily habits.

Each decision—whether in a boardroom, a budget discussion, or a one-on-one meeting—becomes a marker of culture. Over time, these markers form the story of an organization's identity.

Five Daily Habits of Ethical Leaders
1. **Pause Before Deciding:** In a fast-paced environment, leaders feel pressure to decide quickly. But rushing often leads to shortcuts. Ethical leaders create space to evaluate options against values. Even a thirty-second pause to ask, *"Does this align with who we are?"* can prevent costly compromises.
2. **Seek Counsel:** Ethical leaders invite trusted peers, advisors, or mentors to weigh in on tough calls. Seeking counsel is not a sign of weakness but of wisdom. It expands perspective, surfaces blind spots, and prevents isolation.
3. **Name the Tension:** Ethical leaders acknowledge out loud the conflict they feel: *"Here's the pressure I feel, but here's the principle that matters more."* Naming the tension does two things—it clarifies priorities for the leader and signals integrity to others. People learn that pressure exists, but values carry more weight.
4. **Document Decisions:** Writing down the rationale behind decisions creates both accountability and reflection. It prevents selective memory, helps leaders revisit their reasoning later, and provides a record if the decision is questioned. Documentation also models transparency.
5. **Teach Ethics Through Example:** Ethics is best taught not in lectures but in lived practice. Leaders allow others to watch them choose principle over popularity, transparency over spin, and integrity over expedience. Every visible decision becomes a lesson for those who follow.

The Cultural Impact of Daily Ethical Practice

I often remind teams: *"Our culture will be defined less by what we say we value and more by what we choose when it's costly."* That truth reframes daily decisions as cultural markers. A culture of integrity is not preserved by posters on the wall but by choices in the moment.

When leaders consistently practice these habits—pausing, seeking counsel, naming tension, documenting decisions, and teaching by example—they normalize ethical decision-making. Over time, these small choices compound into credibility, trust, and legacy.

Holistic leaders understand that ethics becomes culture not through theory but through disciplined practice. Daily integrity, practiced faithfully, ensures that when the big tests come, leaders and teams will be ready to choose courage over compromise.

Building Ethical Cultures, Not Just Ethical Leaders

Strong leaders can inspire ethical choices, but without supportive cultures, even principled individuals will struggle to sustain integrity. Ethics cannot rest on the shoulders of one person—it must be woven into the DNA of the organization. Cultures outlast individual leaders, and when ethics become cultural, trust endures across generations.

Culture is shaped by what leaders reward, tolerate, and reinforce every day. If performance is celebrated while cutting corners is ignored, expedience will become the norm. If integrity is consistently recognized, protected, and modeled, people will internalize that values matter more than convenience.

How Leaders Build Ethical Cultures:

1. **Model from the Top**
   Culture begins with example. People watch what leaders do more than what they say. Executives who disclose conflicts of interest, admit mistakes, and explain the "why" behind tough ethical calls set a tone that filters through every level. Supervisors reinforce this tone when they apply the same standards on the front lines.

2. **Align Systems with Values**
   Systems either reinforce or undermine culture. Performance evaluations, reward structures, and recognition programs should highlight integrity as much as results. If someone delivers outcomes but violates values in the process, culture erodes. Aligning systems ensures that ethics is not optional—it is operational.

3. **Protect Dissent and Transparency**
   Cultures of integrity create safe channels for people to raise concerns. Whistleblower protections, anonymous reporting, and open-door policies make it clear that truth is welcome. Ethical leaders do not punish dissenting voices; they see them as guardrails that prevent drift.

4. **Integrate Ethics into Everyday Processes**
   Make ethics part of decision-making, not an afterthought. Include values-based questions in project proposals, budgeting conversations, and hiring processes. Over time, asking "Does this align with our values?" becomes as natural as asking about cost or timeline.

5. **Celebrate Ethical Wins**
   Too often, organizations only celebrate performance milestones. Ethical cultures also celebrate when someone chooses integrity, even at a cost. Whether it's an employee who turned down a questionable deal or a manager who owned up to a mistake publicly, recognition reinforces that ethics is success.

Example in Practice:
I once worked with a team that added an "ethics moment" to weekly meetings. One person would share a brief story—a decision they faced, a dilemma they navigated, or a value they upheld. At first, the stories were simple, even awkward. But over time, they became powerful testimonies that reinforced shared values. What began as a small ritual shaped the culture more than any formal policy could.

Why Culture Matters
Ethical leaders can set examples, but cultures preserve them. When ethics becomes collective—shaped by shared practices, reinforced by systems, and celebrated openly—it no longer depends on the character of one individual. It becomes the identity of the whole.

Holistic leaders recognize that their role is not only to embody integrity but to embed it. They leave behind more than reputations—they leave behind organizations where ethics outlives them, ensuring that legacy is not tied to one leader but carried forward by many.

Ethical Pitfalls and Best Practices
Pitfall 1: Choosing Expedience Over Integrity
- Example: Approving a cheaper but unsafe option to meet deadlines.
- Best Practice: Ask, "What will this decision signal about our values?"

Pitfall 2: Withholding Truth to Avoid Discomfort
- Example: Softening bad news so it feels less painful.
- Best Practice: Share truth with clarity and compassion. People can handle hard realities if they trust your integrity.

Pitfall 3: Rationalizing "Everyone Does It"
- Example: Justifying unethical behavior because it's common in the industry.
- Best Practice: Anchor decisions in timeless principles, not shifting norms.

Pitfall 4: Ignoring Voices of Dissent
- Example: Moving forward without hearing concerns because they slow things down.
- Best Practice: Create space for disagreement. Dissent often surfaces blind spots.

Pitfall 5: Confusing Silence with Agreement
- Example: Assuming no one objects when, in fact, people fear speaking up.
- Best Practice: Ask directly, "What risks or concerns might we be overlooking?"

Pitfall 6: Confusing legal with ethical
- Best Practice: Go beyond compliance and ask if it's just.

Reflective Questions
1. What pressures most often tempt you to compromise values?
2. Do you make space for dissenting voices in decision-making?
3. How do you test decisions against your values?
4. What systems in your organization support or hinder ethical choices?
5. How do you model moral courage when decisions are unpopular?
6. Where do I most need accountability right now?

Journaling Prompts
- Write about a time you made a difficult ethical decision. What gave you courage?
- Reflect on a situation where silence felt easier. What might you do differently now?
- Journal about the legacy you want your leadership decisions to leave.
- List three practices you will use to strengthen your moral courage this month.

90-Day Ethics and Courage Plan

Month 1 – Awareness
- Identify one area where ethical tension is most common.
- Write down your personal non-negotiable values.
- Share your non-negotiables with a peer for accountability.

Month 2 – Practice
- Apply the Ethics Test to at least one real decision.
- Apply the PLUS model or Legacy Question to a real decision and debrief it with your team

Month 3 – Culture
- Create a space in team meetings for discussing values-based dilemmas.
- Establish one structural safeguard (e.g., decision log, peer review) to anchor culture.

By the end of 90 days, you will not only strengthen your own ethical decision-making but also shape a culture where moral courage is celebrated and practiced.

Ethical leaders are remembered not only for what they achieved but for how they achieved it. Ethical leaders are remembered not only for what they achieved but for how they plant trust and credibility one principled decision at a time.

8 BUILDING CHARACTER AND VIRTUE

Leadership that endures is anchored in character. Skills may open doors, and vision may attract followers, but only virtue sustains trust. When pressure rises, integrity, humility, and courage determine whether influence deepens or dissolves. This chapter explores why character is leadership's true currency and how virtue becomes the engine of legacy.

Why Virtue Matters in Leadership
Skill opens the door to leadership, but character determines whether you stay there. We may admire competence, but we trust character.

Leadership, at its deepest level, is a moral act. People follow leaders not only because of their strategies or intelligence but because of who they are. We may admire competence, but we trust character. True legacy-minded leadership requires character — the inner compass that guides decisions when no one is watching.

Holistic leadership emphasizes that leadership is not only about results but also about the process of achieving them. A leader who accomplishes goals by cutting corners, manipulating others, or sacrificing integrity will eventually lose trust. By contrast, leaders who consistently embody virtue — honesty, courage, humility, and integrity — inspire loyalty and create cultures where trust thrives.

Character is not something leaders either have or lack. It is cultivated over time through discipline, reflection, and practice. Like muscles, virtues grow stronger with consistent exercise. This chapter explores five essential virtues of leadership — integrity, honesty, servitude, purpose, and discipline — and offers practical ways to strengthen them in everyday leadership. Character is built daily, not granted instantly.

The Virtue Gap: What Happens When Character is Missing

Leadership without virtue is impressive but unstable—eventually cracks appear. Skills, strategy, and even vision cannot sustain leadership if the underlying character is weak. This is the **virtue gap** — the space between a leader's ability and their integrity.

When the virtue gap widens, three predictable outcomes emerge:

1. **Erosion of Trust**
   Followers may admire competence, but they place their loyalty in character. A leader who bends truth, breaks promises, or cuts corners sends a signal that people cannot rely on their word. Once trust is broken, even exceptional results cannot rebuild it easily. Followers begin to question not just decisions, but motives.
2. **Cultural Fragmentation**
   Organizations mirror their leaders. When leaders model inconsistency or dishonesty, the culture learns to do the same. Small compromises become normalized: expense reports padded, deadlines extended without accountability, inclusion ignored. Over time, these fractures multiply into silos, conflict, and disengagement.
3. **Short-Term Wins, Long-Term Collapse**
   Leaders without virtue may achieve success in the short run. They may drive revenue, secure promotions, or attract followers. But without integrity and purpose anchoring those successes, they fail to endure. Teams burn out, reputations tarnish, and legacies are lost.

The virtue gap often begins subtly. It rarely starts with a major ethical breach. Instead, it grows in the small compromises: *the unkept promise, the unspoken truth, the convenient excuse.* Over time, these small cracks widen until credibility is fractured.

By contrast, when leaders close the virtue gap through integrity, honesty, servitude, purpose, and discipline, their influence compounds. Followers know what to expect. They see consistency between words and actions. They learn that even under pressure, their leader's compass will not waver. That consistency builds a culture of trust that multiplies impact far beyond the leader's individual capacity.

The Virtues of Holistic Leadership
These five virtues form the backbone of holistic leadership.
- **Integrity:** Consistency between words and actions.
- **Honesty:** Commitment to truth, even when uncomfortable.
- **Servanthood:** Placing others' growth and well-being above personal ambition.
- **Purpose:** Anchoring daily actions in mission and meaning.
- **Discipline:** Practicing consistency and follow-through, especially under pressure.

Integrity: The Foundation of Trust
Without integrity, no amount of talent, vision, or charisma can sustain influence. Integrity means consistency between values and actions — doing what you say you will do, even when it is difficult or costly.

Integrity is tested most under pressure. Anyone can lead with values when resources are abundant and choices are easy. The real test comes when shortcuts tempt, when competitors press, or when results could be improved if principles were bent. Leaders with integrity resist those temptations and model consistency.

I recall being in a meeting where a faster path was proposed — one that would save time but compromise standards. It was tempting to agree, but I knew the long-term cost would outweigh the short-term benefit. I said, *"If we make this decision, we may solve today's problem, but we'll create a precedent that erodes trust tomorrow. It's not worth it."* It wasn't the popular stance, but it was the right one. That decision set a tone for the team: values would not be sacrificed for expedience.

Building Integrity
1. **Keep Commitments Small and Specific.** Avoid overpromising. Deliver consistently on what you commit.
2. **Model Transparency.** Admit mistakes quickly rather than concealing them.
3. **Create a Personal Integrity Statement.** Write down your non-negotiables and revisit them monthly.
4. **Audit Your Actions.** Weekly, ask: *Did my actions align with my stated values?*

Honesty: Leading with Truth

Honesty is more than the absence of lies; it is the practice of openness and truth-telling. Leaders who communicate honestly build credibility. Leaders who withhold, distort, or mislead may enjoy temporary compliance but forfeit trust.

In one workgroup, I faced the temptation to soften difficult news to maintain morale. Instead, I chose honesty: *"This is going to be challenging. It will stretch us. But here's why it's worth it, and here's how we'll support one another."* To my surprise, honesty didn't deflate the group — it empowered them. People respond better to truth paired with clarity than to hollow reassurance.

Building Honesty
1. **Deliver Truth with Care.** Frame honesty with empathy and respect.
2. **Normalize Limits.** Say, *"I don't know yet, but I'll find out."*
3. **Reward Candor.** Acknowledge and thank those who speak honestly.
4. **Check for Motives.** Before speaking, ask: *Am I sharing this to serve the mission or myself?*

Honesty earns trust; servitude channels that trust into growth.

Servant Leadership: Strength Through Service

Servant leadership reframes the role of leaders: followers do not exist to serve leaders; leaders exist to serve followers. Servitude is not weakness but strength expressed through humility. Leaders who prioritize the growth and well-being of their teams build loyalty and resilience.

I remember leading a project where the workload was overwhelming. I could have insisted that the team simply work harder, but instead I asked: *"What do you need from me to be successful?"* That question created space for honesty. Some needed clarity, others resources, and one encouragement. By addressing those needs, I empowered the team to thrive. Servant leadership removes barriers so people can rise to the standard.

Building Servant Leadership
1. **Ask Before Directing.** *"What do you need to succeed?"*
2. **Celebrate Contributions.** Recognize effort, not only results.
3. **Mentor Intentionally.** Invest in one or two people deeply each year.
4. **Adopt a "You First" Mentality.** Allow others to speak before you in meetings.

Servant leaders remove obstacles so others can excel.

Purpose: Anchoring Leadership in Meaning

Purpose provides the compass for leadership. Without it, leaders may achieve goals but eventually drift. Purpose answers the deeper question: *Why do I lead?* When leaders embody purpose, they inspire others. Purpose transforms daily tasks into meaningful contributions.

During a season of heavy workload, I noticed morale declining. Meetings had become mechanical, energy drained. I stopped and said, *"I know this feels overwhelming, but remember why we're doing this. It isn't just about finishing tasks. It's about leaving something behind that will serve others long after we're gone."* The atmosphere shifted. Purpose breathed life back into the room.

Building Purpose
1. **Write a Mission Statement.** Capture why you lead and what legacy you want to leave.
2. **Align Purpose with Practice.** Audit your calendar — does it reflect your priorities?
3. **Communicate Purpose Often.** Repeat the "why" until it becomes culture.
4. **Anchor Decisions in Purpose.** Ask: *Does this choice serve our deeper mission?*

Purpose fuels perseverance; discipline keeps it burning.

Discipline: Staying the Course

Discipline is consistency — doing what is necessary even when it isn't easy. Leadership often involves fatigue, distractions, and competing priorities. Discipline sustains progress when excitement fades.

I once led a project that stretched for months. Halfway through, energy waned. I committed to modeling discipline: arriving prepared, following through on commitments, staying consistent even when I was tired. My consistency reignited theirs. Discipline is contagious.

Building Discipline
1. **Create Rhythms.** Establish daily habits like journaling, reflection, or reading.
2. **Use Accountability.** Share goals with a peer who will follow up.
3. **Practice Sacrifice.** Choose one comfort to forgo each month in pursuit of growth.
4. **Celebrate Progress.** Acknowledge milestones, even small ones.
5. **Reset Regularly.** Pause quarterly to realign effort with mission.

Integrating the Virtues

Integrity binds, honesty clarifies, servitude humbles, purpose directs, discipline sustains. Honesty ensures transparency. Servitude roots leadership in humility. Purpose provides direction. Discipline sustains action.

I once guided a group through a tough season where all five virtues were required. Integrity demanded we reject shortcuts. Honesty required me to share the truth even when it was hard. Servitude meant asking what people needed from me rather than what I demanded from them. Purpose gave us vision. Discipline carried us through fatigue. In the end, the project succeeded not because of talent alone but because character was present in every decision.

The discipline of showing up consistently, speaking truthfully, and keeping commitments creates the soil from which legacy grows. Leaders who embody these virtues achieve more than results; they shape cultures of trust and leave legacies that last. Holding virtues in balance keeps strength from becoming distortion.

Virtues in Tension: Balancing Strengths Without Compromise

Virtue in leadership is not static; it lives in dynamic tension. Each virtue, when overextended or isolated from the others, can distort into a weakness. Effective leaders recognize that virtues must work together, balanced in practice and reinforced by context.

1. **Integrity vs. Pragmatism**
   Integrity demands adherence to principles, but leadership often unfolds in messy, imperfect environments. The temptation arises to compromise "just this once" for expediency. Too rigid an application of integrity without sensitivity to context can appear inflexible, while pragmatism without integrity erodes credibility.
   Balance Point: Ask not just "What works?" but "What works without violating our values?" Integrity provides the non-negotiable boundaries within which pragmatic decisions can still adapt to real-world challenges.

2. **Honesty vs. Discretion**
   Leaders are called to be transparent, but complete openness without discernment can overwhelm or harm. For example, sharing unfiltered fears with a team can create panic instead of trust. On the other hand, withholding too much information creates suspicion.
   Balance Point: Honesty must be paired with empathy and wisdom. Share truth in ways that serve people, not burden them. The measure is whether communication builds clarity and trust, not simply whether all details are revealed.
3. **Servitude vs. Authority**
   Servant leadership prioritizes meeting the needs of others. Yet leaders must also exercise authority to guide, correct, and make difficult calls. Overemphasizing servitude can drift into passivity, while overemphasizing authority risks dominance.
   Balance Point: Servant leadership does not abdicate authority; it reframes it. Authority is exercised *for* people, not *over* them. True service sometimes means making hard decisions for the well-being of the whole.
4. **Purpose vs. Pressure**
   Purpose anchors leadership in meaning, but the pressure of urgent demands can easily overshadow long-term vision. Leaders who focus only on purpose may appear idealistic, while those who focus only on pressure-driven results risk burnout and cynicism.
   Balance Point: Purpose should not remove urgency; it should redefine it. Urgent tasks are framed as steps toward meaningful outcomes, turning pressure into fuel rather than distraction.
5. **Discipline vs. Flexibility**
   Discipline sustains progress, but rigid discipline can stifle creativity. On the other hand, flexibility without discipline drifts into inconsistency. ***Balance Point:*** Discipline provides the structure, while flexibility allows adaptation. A disciplined leader says, "We will show up prepared every week," but also creates space to adjust when new realities arise.

These tensions do not mean leaders must choose between virtues. Instead, they invite leaders to practice discernment — holding virtues in relationship with one another. Legacy-minded leaders learn to navigate these tensions without abandoning core values.

Virtue in Decision-Making

Every leadership decision carries weight beyond the immediate outcome. Decisions shape culture, communicate values, and set precedents. Over time, they become the story of a leader's character. This is why virtue cannot remain an abstract idea; it must be applied directly in the process of making choices.

A purely technical decision may achieve short-term efficiency, but a virtuous decision asks: *What will this communicate about who we are?* Legacy-minded leaders recognize that how a decision is made often matters as much as what decision is made.

The Four Filters of Virtuous Decision-Making
1. **Integrity Filter** – *Does this align with our values?* If a decision requires compromise on integrity, it is not sustainable. Even small breaches set dangerous precedents. The integrity filter ensures that actions remain consistent with the leader's stated commitments and organizational identity.
2. **Honesty Filter** – *Am I being transparent in this choice?* Leaders must assess whether they are presenting the situation truthfully to those affected. Honesty builds trust even when the outcome is difficult. Without it, leaders risk creating a culture of suspicion.
3. **Servitude Filter** – *Who benefits, and who bears the cost?* Decisions are never neutral. Virtuous leaders ask whether the choice truly serves the people entrusted to them, rather than advancing personal ambition or short-term optics.
4. **Purpose and Discipline Filter** – *Does this decision advance our mission, and will we follow through?* Purpose ensures decisions point toward the legacy the leader hopes to leave. Discipline ensures those decisions are acted upon with consistency, not abandoned when enthusiasm fades.

When values filter every decision, virtue becomes a system, not a speech.

Preventing Ethical Drift
Many leaders do not fail in virtue because of one dramatic decision but because of a series of small compromises — "ethical drift." Each shortcut, half-truth, or neglected commitment gradually reshapes culture until the organization no longer recognizes itself. Virtuous decision-making prevents drift by making values explicit in every process.

When facing a significant decision, leaders can adopt a *Virtue Audit*:
- Write the decision at the top of a page.
- Underneath, create five columns labeled **Integrity, Honesty, Servitude, Purpose, and Discipline.**
- For each, ask: *How does this decision uphold or compromise this virtue?*
- If any column raises red flags, pause. Consider alternatives or mitigating steps before proceeding.

This exercise turns virtue from abstraction into practice. Over time, teams begin to expect these filters in conversations, creating shared accountability for virtuous decision-making.

Why It Matters
Virtuous decision-making builds resilience. Organizations led this way can weather crises, because followers trust that even in pressure, their leaders will choose integrity over expedience, honesty over comfort, service over ego, purpose over distraction, and discipline over fatigue.

Leaders who consistently run decisions through these filters not only protect their own credibility but also teach their teams to lead in the same way. This is how character becomes culture, and culture becomes legacy.

Cultivating Virtue in Teams
Virtue in leadership is not only an individual pursuit; it is a collective practice. A leader's character sets the tone, but culture determines whether virtue is reinforced or eroded. Teams thrive when integrity, honesty, servitude, purpose, and discipline are not merely traits of the leader but shared commitments embraced by everyone.

Building virtue in teams requires intentional design. Trust and integrity do not emerge by accident; they are cultivated through practices, rituals, and reinforcement. When teams adopt virtues as shared values, the result is not just compliance but cohesion — a community bound together by principles that outlast immediate goals.

1. Define Shared Values Clearly

Too often, organizations post values on walls but fail to translate them into behaviors. Teams need clarity on what each virtue looks like in practice. For example:

- Integrity: "We follow through on what we commit, even in small tasks."
- Honesty: "We share concerns openly and respectfully."
- Servitude: "We look for ways to make one another's work easier."
- Purpose: "We remind ourselves of why our work matters."
- Discipline: "We uphold routines and standards, even under pressure."

When values are linked to specific, observable actions, team members can hold themselves and each other accountable without ambiguity.

2. Model and Mirror Virtue

Leaders shape team culture by what they tolerate, celebrate, and practice. A single compromise on integrity — like overlooking a missed commitment or brushing off an exaggeration — can ripple through the team. Conversely, consistent modeling reinforces that virtues matter. When a leader keeps promises, admits mistakes, or practices discipline under pressure, the team mirrors those behaviors. Virtue is contagious when it is visible.

3. Create Structures of Accountability

Virtue requires reinforcement. Teams can use practical tools such as:

- **Team Integrity Ledger**: A collective record of commitments made and fulfilled.
- **Values-to-Behavior Mapping**: Defining how each team value translates into specific actions.
- **Feedback Rhythms**: Quarterly sessions where team members reflect on how well they are living shared virtues.

These structures make virtue measurable and visible, preventing it from remaining abstract. Structures turn intent into habit.

4. Normalize Servant Practices

Servitude in teams is not just about leaders serving followers; it is about teammates serving one another. Simple practices — like asking, "What do you need from me to succeed this week?" — foster humility and collaboration. Over time, these small acts of service create a culture where people feel supported, not used.

5. Anchor in Collective Purpose

Teams that regularly revisit their shared purpose stay resilient in the face of setbacks. Purpose unifies effort, transforms conflict into collaboration, and reminds people that they are contributing to something larger than themselves. Anchoring virtue in purpose ensures that the team does not just meet objectives but builds legacy together.

6. Celebrate Virtue Publicly

Recognition matters. When a team member demonstrates integrity, honesty, or discipline, leaders should highlight it in meetings or reports. Celebration reinforces what the group values most. Over time, people associate virtue with honor and belonging, rather than obligation.

Why This Matters

When teams embody virtue collectively, culture shifts from fragile to resilient. Integrity becomes the norm, honesty becomes safe, service becomes natural, purpose becomes energizing, and discipline becomes shared. In such an environment, legacy is not dependent on a single leader. It becomes embedded in the team's identity, ensuring that even as people come and go, the culture of virtue endures.

The Long View: Virtue and Legacy

Virtue in leadership is not only about today's decisions; it is about tomorrow's memory. Leaders may be celebrated for results in the short term, but over time, what endures is how those results were achieved and the character displayed in achieving them. Legacy is built not in the headlines of the moment but in the quiet consistency of a life lived with integrity, honesty, servitude, purpose, and discipline.

When leaders focus only on immediate outcomes, they risk compromising values for speed, profit, or popularity. But legacy-minded leaders adopt the long view. They recognize that every small choice is a seed planted. Integrity today yields trust tomorrow. Honesty in a difficult moment creates credibility that will be remembered for years. Servitude shapes cultures where people thrive long after the leader is gone. Purpose infuses work with meaning that inspires the next generation. Discipline ensures that these virtues are not occasional flashes of brilliance but steady patterns that shape culture over decades.

Taking the long view requires leaders to ask: *How will this decision be remembered ten years from now? What precedent does it set? Does it reflect the kind of leader I aspire to be?* These questions move leadership beyond expedience into significance. They remind leaders that the story told about their leadership will not be written only in quarterly reports or annual reviews but in the lives of the people they influence.

Virtue as Legacy Multiplier

- **Integrity** ensures that trust compounds. Each kept promise builds credibility, and credibility multiplies influence.
- **Honesty** prevents the erosion of trust, ensuring that the truth anchors culture long after leaders have moved on.
- **Servitude** multiplies leaders by developing others, embedding a legacy of service into organizational DNA.
- **Purpose** keeps vision alive, outlasting the leader and guiding successors.
- **Discipline** sustains momentum, ensuring that noble intentions translate into consistent results.

A Legacy Perspective

Consider two leaders with equal talent and strategy. One compromises values to achieve quick wins; the other remains steadfast to principle, even at a cost. In the short term, both may appear successful. But years later, the difference is stark: one is remembered with regret, the other with respect.

Followers may forget details of plans or projects, but they never forget how a leader made them feel and the virtues that leader embodied.

Practical Practices for the Long View
1. **Legacy Journaling** – Weekly, reflect on the question: "What will this week's decisions say about my character five years from now?"
2. **Mentorship Investment** – Dedicate time to developing others, ensuring that your values live beyond your tenure.
3. **Quarterly Legacy Summaries** – Document where virtues guided decisions, where compromises were resisted, and where growth is still needed.
4. **Succession with Integrity** – Prepare others not only to take your role but to carry your values. Passing on virtue is the essence of legacy.

Why It Matters
Leadership divorced from virtue may win for the moment, but it cannot endure. The long view requires patience, humility, and courage. It asks leaders to resist the seduction of applause today for the sake of honor tomorrow. In the end, the question is not only, *What did I achieve?* but, *What did I leave behind?* Virtue ensures that the answer is more than accomplishments — it is a legacy of trust, service, and meaning that outlives the leader.

Pitfalls & Best Practices
Pitfall 1: Confusing Charisma for Character
- Example: Following a leader for charm, only to be disappointed in inconsistency.
- Best Practice: Evaluate leaders by integrity and consistency, not popularity.

Pitfall 2: Compartmentalizing Values
- Example: Acting ethically at work but cutting corners in personal life.
- Best Practice: Practice wholeness; live the same values everywhere.

Pitfall 3: Prioritizing Results Over Relationships
- Example: Driving for outcomes but neglecting people's well-being.
- Best Practice: Balance accountability with care.

Pitfall 4: Assuming Character is Fixed
- Example: Believing that once you have integrity, it requires no effort.
- Best Practice: Practice virtues daily; character is strengthened over time.

Pitfall 5: Neglecting Small Choices
- Example: Dismissing "little lies" or broken promises as insignificant.
- Best Practice: Remember, small cracks widen; integrity is built in the details.

Pitfall 6: Preaching Virtue Without Practicing It
- Best Practice: Model first, teach later.

Reflective Questions
1. When was the last time you kept a commitment under pressure?
2. Do you find it easier to share difficult truths or to avoid them?
3. How do you serve your team beyond their performance metrics?
4. What is your personal leadership purpose?
5. Where in your life is discipline most needed?

Journaling Prompts
- Reflect on a moment when honesty deepened trust.
- Journal about your purpose and how it has shifted over time.
- Record one discipline you want to strengthen this month.
- Reflect on one area where your actions and words may not fully align.
- List three daily choices this week that demonstrated your values.

90-Day Character Growth Plan

Month 1 – Integrity and Honesty
- Write about a time when your integrity was tested. How did you respond?
- Journal about a leader whose character shaped you. What specific virtues did they model?
- Reflect on one area where your actions and words may not fully align.
- Write a personal integrity statement.
- Deliver one difficult truth with empathy.

Month 2 – Servitude and Purpose
- Ask three people: *"How can I serve you better?"*
- Draft or refine your personal mission statement.
- Track how often you act on your mission statement.

Month 3 – Discipline
- Choose one value and practice aligning your daily actions with it.
- Choose one new daily habit aligned with your purpose.
- Track progress weekly with an accountability partner.

By the end of 90 days, you will not only clarify your values but also weave them into your leadership practices, shaping both your culture and your legacy.

When the story of your leadership is told, people may remember your strategies or your successes, but what will endure is your character. Virtue is the foundation of legacy — because legacy is not only what you build, but who you become. Values are proven under pressure. Character forms the core of legacy; next, we turn to resilience—the virtue that keeps leaders standing when pressure returns.

9 LEADING THROUGH ADVERSITY

Every leader will face storms. Some will shrink back, retreating in fear or paralysis. Others will push forward recklessly, driving progress at the expense of their people. But resilient leaders find a third way: they lead with steadiness and foster renewal. They neither deny the difficulty nor crush others beneath it. Instead, they model courage, honesty, and discipline that carry people through hardship with dignity and hope.

Resilience is the capacity to endure. It is the ability to remain steady when circumstances shake, to adapt when plans collapse, and to persevere when pressure mounts. Renewal is the discipline to restore. It is the intentional practice of recharging energy, refreshing perspective, and reconnecting to purpose so that resilience is sustainable. Together, resilience and renewal ensure that adversity does not end a leader's influence but strengthens it.

This balance matters because resilience without renewal leads to burnout, while renewal without resilience produces fragility. Leaders who only "power through" eventually collapse under exhaustion. Leaders who only retreat into recovery never grow the stamina to endure. Legacy-minded leaders understand that storms are not detours but defining moments. They cultivate both resilience and renewal, demonstrating to their teams that hardship can refine rather than destroy. This chapter shows how leaders hold steady, recover strength, and turn adversity into legacy.

Why Resilience and Renewal Belong Together:
- **Resilience sustains direction.** It keeps leaders moving when obstacles arise.
- **Renewal sustains spirit.** It replenishes energy so resilience does not become brittle.
- **Together, they sustain legacy.** They shape how leaders are remembered—not just for what they achieved, but for how they endured and restored others in the process.

Storms will come—economic downturns, organizational crises, personal setbacks, or unexpected change. What distinguishes enduring leaders is not the absence of hardship but the way they navigate it. Followers will forget many strategic details, but they will remember how their leader carried them through the storm—with panic, with pressure, or with steady resilience paired with genuine renewal.

Holistic leaders choose the third way. They stand firm in values, invite honesty in struggle, and build rhythms of recovery that keep both themselves and their people healthy. In doing so, they not only weather adversity but also strengthen the trust, courage, and hope that will carry their legacy forward.

Holding Steady Through the Storm

The room was heavy with silence. The team had been working relentlessly on a project that stretched far beyond its original timeline. Deadlines kept shifting, expectations kept growing, and morale was wearing thin. I could see the fatigue in their faces—the kind of weariness that isn't solved by another pep talk or a motivational slogan. They didn't need more pressure; they required resilience.

In that moment, I chose honesty over hype. I acknowledged what we were all feeling: *"This is hard. It's okay to say we're tired. But I also believe we are stronger than this moment, and we're going to finish together."* Instead of driving them harder, I created space for them to exhale. I invited frustrations into the room and listened as people named their struggles. Then I reassured them that fatigue didn't mean failure—it meant they were stretching, growing, and being refined by the challenge. By normalizing the struggle, I gave them permission to breathe. Finally, I anchored us again in purpose, reminding them why the work mattered and how it connected to something larger than the deadlines pressing in on us. People rarely need louder motivation; they need visible steadiness.

Why Steadiness Matters in Storms

Leaders cannot always change circumstances, but they can influence how people experience them. When storms rise:

- **Some leaders panic,** amplifying fear in the room.
- **Others push relentlessly,** driving people to exhaustion.
- **Resilient leaders hold steady,** calming the environment and renewing perspective.

Steadiness is not about pretending the storm doesn't exist; it is about being the calm within it. Teams look to leaders for cues. If the leader collapses under pressure, so will the team. If the leader ignores the reality of fatigue, the team will feel unseen. But when the leader acknowledges difficulty with honesty and anchors people in hope, resilience begins to take root.

Practical Steadiness Habits:
1. **Name the Reality.** Say out loud what people are already feeling. This validates their experience and builds trust.
2. **Normalize the Struggle.** Remind the team that fatigue and setbacks are part of growth, not signs of failure.
3. **Listen Before Directing.** Give people a chance to voice frustrations before offering solutions.
4. **Re-anchor in Purpose.** Point back to the "why" behind the work. Meaning sustains energy when momentum falters.
5. **Model Calm.** Your tone, posture, and words can either amplify stress or create space for renewal.

For Leaders at All Levels:
- A **supervisor** may reassure a frontline team that their effort is noticed and valued, even when goals feel overwhelming.
- A **manager** may facilitate an honest team conversation, helping people process frustration while keeping focus on the mission.
- An **executive** may communicate transparently during organizational crises, acknowledging uncertainty while reaffirming commitment to values.

Storms are inevitable, but panic and pressure are optional. Leaders who choose steadiness help their teams see that resilience is possible. Renewal doesn't come from pretending the storm isn't real—it comes from creating space for honesty, anchoring in purpose, and moving forward together.

The Nature of Resilience in Leadership

Resilience isn't about appearing unshaken; it's honest endurance with purpose. In leadership, resilience is not simply a personal trait reserved for the strong-willed; it is a discipline that can be cultivated, refined, and modeled over time. Resilient leaders provide something priceless when storms rise: stability. They do not deny difficulty, but they do not collapse beneath it either. Instead, they help others find courage when they might otherwise falter. Teams take their cues from their leader—if the leader steadies, the team steadies. Resilience becomes contagious when it is lived consistently.

Angela Duckworth describes resilience as "grit": passion and perseverance over the long haul. Talent may open doors, but grit is what keeps leaders walking through them when setbacks mount. Grit is not stubbornness; it is sustained commitment to meaningful goals, fueled by conviction rather than ego.

Ronald Heifetz's framework of adaptive leadership adds another layer. Resilience is not only about solving technical problems—those with clear solutions—but also about helping people adapt emotionally to loss, change, and uncertainty. A resilient leader does not rush to fix everything; they create conditions where people can process grief, reframe obstacles, and discover new ways forward. This makes resilience both a strategy and a source of emotional strength.

What Resilience Looks Like in Leadership:
- **Acknowledging struggle without surrendering to it.** Leaders say, *"Yes, this is difficult,"* but also, *"We will endure."*
- **Maintaining composure under pressure.** Not because they feel no fear, but because they refuse to let fear lead.
- **Adapting in real time.** When one plan collapses, they do not cling to it out of pride—they adjust and invite others into the learning process.
- **Anchoring in values.** Resilient leaders measure progress not only by outcomes but by how faithfully values are upheld through hardship.

Resilience shows calm in chaos; renewal keeps that calm alive.

For holistic leaders, resilience is not about appearing unshaken or projecting invulnerability. That façade only breeds isolation and pressure. True resilience is about being honest with the struggle while still choosing to move forward, anchored in values. People trust leaders who are both real about challenges and resolute in hope.

But resilience alone is not enough. Renewal is its essential companion—the discipline of restoring energy, vision, and perspective so that resilience remains sustainable, not forced. Resilience without renewal leads to burnout: the leader keeps pushing but eventually breaks. Renewal without resilience creates fragility: the leader feels refreshed but lacks the stamina to endure. Legacy-minded leaders practice both, demonstrating stamina in hardship and rhythms of recovery that make leadership not just possible but sustainable.

For Leaders at All Levels:
- A **supervisor** demonstrates resilience by acknowledging the strain of long shifts but still encouraging the team with steady presence.
- A **manager** models renewal by scheduling reflection sessions after high-pressure projects so the team can process and reset.
- An **executive** shows resilience and renewal together by leading through crisis with calm clarity while also encouraging recovery practices across the organization.

Storms will come. Resilience allows leaders to endure them; renewal allows leaders to emerge from them stronger. Together, they form the foundation of leadership that not only survives but also leaves a legacy of steadiness, courage, and hope.

Personal Resilience: Leading Yourself First

You can't give steadiness that you don't possess. Lead yourself before leading others. Teams draw strength from what their leaders model, and a leader who is depleted cannot offer steadiness to those depending on them. Personal resilience is the foundation of collective resilience. It begins with leading yourself well—managing your energy, mindset, and rhythms so that you can endure and renew with integrity.

Resilience as Self-Leadership

Resilience is not about pretending to be invincible. It is about learning to manage your own fears, fatigue, and frustrations in ways that keep you anchored in purpose. Leaders who push endlessly without reflection may appear strong for a season, but eventually cracks show—often in health, relationships, or judgment. True resilience means knowing when to press forward and when to step back, when to speak strength and when to admit need.

For me, journaling has been one of the simplest but most powerful practices. Writing allows me to process emotions, clarify thoughts, and name challenges for what they are. It transforms vague anxieties into concrete reflections I can learn from. Reflection gives me the distance to see the bigger picture, which often reveals that what feels overwhelming today is shaping tomorrow's growth.

Rest is equally vital. Fatigue distorts perspective, making challenges seem larger and options seem smaller. I intentionally schedule breaks, protect time for renewal, and set boundaries that guard my energy. These rhythms are not indulgence; they are discipline. Rest ensures that resilience is sustainable.

Reframing Challenges

Another key to personal resilience is reframing adversity. Instead of asking, *"Why is this happening to me?"* I ask, *"What is this teaching me? How will this shape me as a leader?"* That shift turns obstacles into opportunities. It doesn't erase difficulty, but it transforms the narrative from one of defeat to one of growth.

Personal Practices for Resilience

1. **Journaling:** Write daily or weekly reflections on challenges and the lessons they bring.
2. **Rest:** Protect sleep and build recovery into your schedule. Treat renewal as essential, not optional.
3. **Reframing:** Ask what the challenge makes possible, not only what it takes away.

4. **Boundaries:** Set limits on availability to preserve focus, family, and health.
5. **Reflection:** Step back regularly to assess progress and adjust course with clarity.

I once entered a season where the pace of leadership was relentless—deadlines, meetings, and demands stacked endlessly. At first, I tried to power through, believing that endurance meant ignoring limits. But I quickly realized that exhaustion was clouding my judgment and shortening my patience. I chose instead to create daily space for reflection and weekly space for rest. The external demands didn't disappear, but my ability to face them improved dramatically. My steadiness as a leader returned not because the storm lessened, but because I had restored my strength within it.

Why Personal Resilience Matters for Legacy
- Teams take their cue from their leader's steadiness.
- Personal rhythms set cultural precedents—if leaders neglect rest, teams will too.
- A leader who endures without renewal leaves behind exhaustion; a leader who pairs resilience with renewal leaves behind sustainability.

Holistic leaders understand this: leading yourself first is not selfish; it is stewardship. When leaders discipline themselves to renew and reframe, they model a way of leading that does not collapse under pressure but thrives through it. In the end, legacy is not built by leaders who burn out quickly but by those who endure steadily, anchored in purpose, and renewed in strength.

Frameworks for Resilience and Renewal
Frameworks translate endurance into repeatable rhythm. Resilience and renewal are powerful ideas, but they do not become reality without structure. Leaders need practical models that translate principles into action—frameworks that can guide how they think, decide, and lead when pressure is high. These frameworks provide language, discipline, and tools for sustaining resilience in both individuals and teams. They remind us that resilience is not accidental; it is cultivated. Renewal is not optional; it is designed. By exploring these models, leaders at every level can anchor their leadership in practices that endure long after the storm has passed.

Grit: Passion and Perseverance Over the Long Haul
While talent and opportunity may open doors, it is grit that keeps leaders walking through them when progress slows or setbacks mount. Grit is not about raw toughness; it is about sustained commitment to meaningful goals.

The Nature of Grit in Leadership

Leaders often start strong, fueled by excitement or urgency. But grit is measured not in beginnings but in endurance. When the applause fades, when results take longer than expected, or when setbacks create discouragement, grit is what keeps leaders moving forward. Teams watch closely in these moments. If their leader falters, they falter. If their leader perseveres with steady conviction, they find the courage to do the same.

What Grit Looks Like in Practice:
- **Consistency:** Showing up day after day, even when motivation wanes.
- **Conviction:** Staying anchored in purpose when external pressures push for shortcuts.
- **Adaptability:** Adjusting strategies without abandoning the mission.
- **Hope:** Believing that effort will matter, even if results take time.

Why Grit Matters for Leaders at All Levels:
- A **supervisor** demonstrates grit when they continue coaching team members even after repeated mistakes, trusting that growth takes time.
- A **manager** shows grit by guiding a department through a tough quarter with transparency and steadiness rather than panic.
- An **executive** embodies grit by staying true to a long-term vision despite external pressures for short-term results.

Balancing Grit with Renewal

Grit without renewal becomes stubbornness that exhausts both leader and team. Renewal ensures that perseverance is fueled by clarity and energy, not mere willpower. Resilient leaders pair grit with practices of rest, reflection, and celebration, ensuring their endurance is sustainable.

The Legacy of Grit

Leaders remembered for grit are those who refused to give up when progress was slow or adversity was fierce. Their legacy is not only in the outcomes they achieved but in the cultures they built—teams and organizations that learned to keep going when others would have quit.

Holistic leaders embody grit not by clinging stubbornly to tasks, but by persevering faithfully toward values and vision. In doing so, they teach others that storms can delay progress but cannot defeat purpose. But grit alone can harden; renewal softens it back into strength.

Adaptive Leadership: Resilience in Times of Change

Ronald Heifetz's framework of adaptive leadership reminds us that resilience is not only about withstanding hardship but also about helping people grow through it. Technical problems—those with clear solutions—can often be resolved with expertise and quick fixes. Adaptive challenges, however, are different. They involve shifts in identity, values, or ways of working. They cannot be solved by knowledge alone; they require learning, experimentation, and emotional resilience.

The Core of Adaptive Leadership

Adaptive leadership emphasizes balancing stability with flexibility. Resilient leaders acknowledge that while circumstances may change, values and mission remain steady. They reassure people that the foundation is secure while also inviting them to adapt how they think and act. This balance allows teams to navigate uncertainty without losing trust or direction.

What Adaptive Leadership Looks Like:

- **Naming Reality Honestly.** Instead of minimizing difficulty, adaptive leaders tell the truth about the challenge while framing it as an opportunity for growth.
- **Creating Safe Spaces.** They build environments where teams can experiment, fail forward, and learn without fear of shame or punishment.
- **Resisting the Urge to Provide All the Answers.** Instead of rushing to fix everything, adaptive leaders mobilize the collective wisdom of their teams.
- **Modeling Flexibility.** They show that adjusting course is not weakness but wisdom.

For Leaders at All Levels:

- A **supervisor** practices adaptive leadership by helping team members adjust to a new process, giving space for questions and concerns instead of expecting instant compliance.
- A **manager** models adaptive leadership when guiding a department through restructuring, balancing honest acknowledgment of loss with reassurance about shared mission.
- An **executive** embodies adaptive leadership by steering the organization through cultural shifts, such as embracing diversity or sustainability, framing change as an opportunity for growth rather than a threat.

The Legacy of Adaptive Leadership

Adaptive leaders are remembered not for solving every problem but for equipping people to grow through change. They leave behind cultures that are resilient not only in surviving disruption but in thriving because of it. By teaching people how to adapt without losing identity, they create organizations that endure long after their tenure.

Holistic leaders understand that resilience is not about clinging rigidly to the past but about holding fast to values while learning how to navigate the future. Adaptive leadership ensures that storms do not just test resilience—they strengthen it. Adaptive leaders make growth the outcome of every disruption.

Energy Management Model: Sustaining Resilience

Energy, not time, limits resilience. Resilient leaders recognize that time is finite, but energy is renewable. While we cannot create more hours in a day, we can learn to steward and replenish the energy that fuels our leadership. The Energy Management Model teaches that resilience is not about doing more but about sustaining energy across four dimensions: physical, emotional, mental, and spiritual. When one dimension is neglected, the others eventually suffer. Balanced energy allows leaders to endure hardship without losing perspective, health, or hope.

1. Physical Energy: The Foundation of Endurance

Physical energy is the fuel of the body. Without it, even the most passionate leader will falter. Leaders often sacrifice sleep, exercise, and nutrition in the name of productivity, but the cost is clarity and effectiveness.

- **Practices for Renewal:** Prioritize consistent sleep, eat foods that sustain energy rather than drain it, and build movement into your routine. Even a brief walk can restore focus during demanding days.

2. Emotional Energy: The Strength of Relationships

Emotional energy comes from healthy relationships and gratitude. Stress and conflict deplete it; connection and encouragement replenish it. Leaders who isolate themselves in hard seasons often burn out faster, while those who draw on supportive relationships find steadiness.

- **Practices for Renewal:** Express gratitude daily, nurture trusted friendships, and practice empathy in team interactions.

3. Mental Energy: The Power of Focus and Learning

Mental energy fuels problem-solving, creativity, and adaptability. When leaders are overloaded with distractions, their capacity to think clearly collapses. Resilient leaders guard their focus and create space for learning.

- **Practices for Renewal:** Schedule blocks of uninterrupted work, minimize multitasking, and read or study regularly to stimulate creativity.

4. **Spiritual Energy: The Anchor of Purpose**
Spiritual energy is the deepest source of resilience. It flows from alignment with values and clarity of purpose. When leaders forget *why* they are leading, storms feel heavier. When they remain anchored in mission, even great adversity can be endured with hope.
- **Practices for Renewal:** Begin the day by reconnecting with your purpose, engaging in mindfulness or prayer, and reflecting on whether decisions align with your values.

Why Energy Management Sustains Resilience
- Leaders who neglect physical energy eventually compromise mental clarity.
- Leaders who ignore emotional renewal become cynical and impatient.
- Leaders who lose spiritual energy drift into burnout, even if other areas seem strong.

Balanced energy prevents leaders from trading health for results. Resilient leaders integrate renewal into every dimension, creating rhythms that keep their leadership sustainable. This is not indulgence—it is stewardship. By modeling balanced vitality, leaders show their teams that resilience is not about squeezing out more effort but about leading with wholeness.

Holistic leaders understand that storms will drain energy, but renewal will restore it. By protecting energy in every dimension, they endure hardship with strength and leave behind a legacy not of exhaustion but of vitality, wisdom, and hope.

Turning Adversity into Growth
Resilient leaders do more than endure hardship—they learn from it. Reflection and reframing are two disciplines that transform storms from moments of survival into opportunities for growth. Where some see only obstacles, resilient leaders see classrooms. Where some see failure, resilient leaders uncover lessons that shape stronger futures.

Reflection is the practice of stepping back to examine experiences with honesty and curiosity. Without reflection, leaders risk rushing from one challenge to the next, carrying unresolved fatigue and unlearned lessons. Reflection slows the pace long enough to ask:
- *What actually happened?*
- *How did I respond?*
- *What did I learn about myself, my team, and my leadership?*

This process brings clarity, surfaces patterns, and prevents repeated mistakes. Reflection also builds resilience by reminding leaders that storms, while difficult, are temporary and often transformative.

The Discipline of Reframing

Reframing is the ability to view challenges through a different lens. Instead of asking, *"Why is this happening to me?"* leaders ask, *"What can this teach me? How might this prepare us for the future?"* This shift moves adversity from being an enemy to being a teacher.

Reframing doesn't erase difficulty, but it changes the meaning of the difficulty. A setback becomes a lesson in adaptability. A failure becomes raw material for wisdom. A delay becomes space for reflection and regrouping. Leaders who practice reframing help their teams reinterpret struggles as opportunities for growth rather than as signs of weakness.

Practical Practices for Reflection and Reframing

1. **After-Action Reviews:** Following a project or crisis, gather the team to ask, *"What went well? What was difficult? What did we learn?"*
2. **Reframing Questions:** Ask, *"What strengths emerged in us during this challenge? How will this shape who we are becoming?"*
3. **Mentorship Conversations:** Share struggles with mentors who can help provide new perspectives. Sometimes reframing requires outside wisdom.

Why Reflection and Reframing Build Legacy

- They prevent adversity from becoming wasted pain.
- They shape leaders and teams into wiser, more courageous versions of themselves.
- They turn scars into stories of growth that inspire future leaders.

Holistic leaders understand that storms will leave their mark. The question is whether the mark will be a wound that weakens or a lesson that strengthens. Through reflection and reframing, leaders transform adversity into wisdom, ensuring that challenges do not just test their legacy—they enrich it. Reflection makes hardship useful; reframing makes it hopeful.

Team Resilience: Building Collective Strength

Resilience is not only individual; it is collective. Teams, like leaders, face seasons of pressure, uncertainty, and fatigue. When adversity strikes, the difference between a group that fractures and a group that grows stronger often comes down to how resilience is cultivated within the culture. A resilient team can absorb stress, adapt to change, and emerge more united on the other side.

Why Team Resilience Matters

Organizations rarely fail because of one crisis; they fail because teams lack the collective stamina to endure multiple waves of challenge. Resilient teams know how to bend without breaking, recover without resentment, and adapt without losing sight of their purpose. They understand that adversity is not a detour but part of the journey—and often the place where trust and courage deepen.

I once led a group through a season of constant change. At first, resistance was high, and energy was low. Deadlines shifted, processes changed, and uncertainty lingered. Rather than ignoring the frustration, I brought it into the open: *"This transition is stretching us, and it's normal to feel unsettled. But we are going to face it together."* That transparency made the team feel seen and safe. Over time, their confidence grew—not because the storm disappeared, but because they trusted the process and, more importantly, each other.

For Leaders at All Levels:

- A **supervisor** builds team resilience by listening actively to front-line frustrations and modeling hope without denying reality.
- A **manager** strengthens resilience by encouraging collaboration across silos, helping teams see they are not alone in the struggle.
- An **executive** reinforces resilience by communicating consistently and transparently during times of organizational change.

The Cultural Payoff of Team Resilience

When teams learn to navigate storms together, they develop a collective confidence that lasts beyond the immediate challenge. They remember not only what they overcame but *how* they overcame it—by leaning on each other, staying anchored in purpose, and finding renewal together. That memory becomes part of their identity, strengthening them for future trials.

Resilient leaders know this truth: hardship can divide teams or deepen them. The leader who normalizes struggle, protects safety, and anchors people in purpose demonstrates that adversity does not have to fracture—it can forge. Such leaders leave behind more than results; they leave behind communities of trust and courage that can withstand the storms long after the leader has moved on. Shared endurance becomes shared confidence—the signature of resilient cultures.

Collective Renewal: Restoring Teams After Crisis

Storms don't just impact leaders—they leave a mark on teams as well. After an intense project, organizational change, or season of crisis, teams often experience what I call "leadership fatigue." Even if the mission succeeded, the process can leave people drained. Leaders who ignore this reality risk burning out their teams just as momentum is needed for the next challenge.

Collective renewal is the discipline of helping teams recover together. It is about more than rest; it is about restoring trust, energy, and clarity of purpose after adversity. Just as athletes need recovery days to perform at their peak, teams need intentional rhythms of renewal to sustain long-term effectiveness.

Practices for Collective Renewal:
1. **Debrief with Honesty** – Create space for the team to reflect openly: *"What went well? What was difficult? What do we want to carry forward, and what do we need to release?"* Honest conversations validate struggle and surface lessons.
2. **Rituals of Closure** – Mark the end of a hard season with rituals that allow people to acknowledge effort and transition mentally. This could be a celebration meal, a recognition ceremony, or even a symbolic handoff to the next phase.
3. **Celebrate Progress, Not Just Results** – Recognize perseverance, creativity, and collaboration—not only the final outcome. Teams need to know their resilience mattered as much as their output.
4. **Offer Space to Rest** – Build margin after major projects. Even short recovery periods signal that rest is valued, not just relentless activity.
5. **Reconnect to Purpose** – Renewal is not just about taking a break; it is about remembering why the work matters. Leaders should link the team's effort back to mission, values, and long-term impact.

Recovery cements loyalty; rushing past it erodes it.

Why Collective Renewal Matters:
- It prevents teams from carrying unprocessed fatigue into the next season.
- It strengthens culture by showing that people matter more than projects.
- It transforms crisis into growth, embedding resilience as a shared identity.

Resilient leaders understand that storms can wear people down, but they can also forge teams stronger than before. Renewal ensures that adversity becomes a catalyst for unity, not division. Leaders who guide their teams through recovery leave behind organizations marked by health, trust, and long-term vitality.

The Difference Between Resilience and Burnout
Resilience is often misunderstood. Too many leaders equate resilience with toughness, pushing themselves and their teams harder and longer without pause. But resilience is not about endless endurance—it is about sustainable strength. The opposite of resilience is not weakness; it is burnout.

Burnout is what happens when leaders and teams push forward without renewal. It shows up as exhaustion, cynicism, and a loss of purpose. Productivity may continue for a season, but passion and creativity fade. A burned-out leader may still be present in body but absent in vision, leaving their team without the steady anchor they need.

Resilience, by contrast, is the ability to recover, adapt, and continue forward with clarity and purpose. It is not about ignoring stress but about navigating it with honesty and discipline. Resilient leaders admit when they are tired, create rhythms of renewal, and help their teams find sustainable ways to endure.

Key Differences Between Resilience and Burnout:
- **Energy vs. Exhaustion:** Resilient leaders manage and replenish energy; burned-out leaders run on empty.
- **Perspective vs. Cynicism:** Resilience reframes challenges as growth opportunities; burnout reduces them to meaningless obstacles.
- **Purpose vs. Drift:** Resilience anchors in mission; burnout forgets why the work matters.
- **Sustainability vs. Collapse:** Resilience strengthens over time; burnout erodes trust, health, and culture.

Resilience respects limits; burnout ignores them.

I once worked with a manager who prided themselves on "powering through" every challenge. For a while, the results looked impressive. But over time, their constant pushing without rest drained the team. Morale collapsed, creativity dried up, and eventually the manager themselves had to step away due to exhaustion. By contrast, another leader in the same organization built resilience by creating honest conversations about stress, modeling rest, and reconnecting people to purpose. That team not only survived the same challenges but came out stronger because they practiced renewal alongside perseverance.

Resilient leaders know the difference between pushing harder and leading wiser. They understand that storms will come, but the goal is not to survive them at any cost. The goal is to lead through them in a way that sustains both people and purpose. Burnout depletes legacy; resilience strengthens it.

Practices for Team Resilience
1. **Normalize struggle.** Remind teams that adversity is part of growth.
2. **Create safety.** Make it safe for people to admit fatigue or uncertainty.
3. **Anchor in purpose.** Reconnect challenges to the larger "why."
4. **Celebrate milestones.** Recognize small wins to sustain momentum.
5. **Encourage adaptability.** Frame change as an opportunity for innovation.

Practical Tools for Resilience and Renewal

Reframing Challenges
- **Ask:** *"What is this situation teaching us?"*
- **Ask:** *"What strengths are emerging because of this struggle?"*
- **Ask:** *"How might this prepare us for the future?"*

Renewal Rhythms
- Schedule "pulse checks" to ask how people are doing, not just what they are doing.
- Build in short recovery periods after major projects.
- Encourage individuals to adopt personal renewal practices — journaling, mindfulness, faith, or exercise.

Team Practices
- Hold reflection sessions to capture lessons from adversity.
- Share stories of resilience to remind teams of their capacity.
- Establish rituals of gratitude and recognition during long projects.

Resilience and Legacy

Every leader faces storms, but not every leader responds the same way. Some are swept away by pressure, their leadership unraveling in the face of uncertainty. Others push forward recklessly, sacrificing people for progress. But the leaders who leave the deepest imprint are those who stand firm, guiding their teams with steadiness and hope. The difference is not in the size of the storm—it is in the strength of resilience.

Resilience directly shapes legacy. Followers may forget specific strategies, metrics, or even achievements, but they will always remember how their leader responded under pressure. Did you panic, compromise, or retreat? Or did you acknowledge the challenge honestly, anchor in values, and press forward with steadiness? These moments of pressure become defining stories that are retold long after the crisis has ended.

Why Resilience Shapes Legacy:
- **It builds trust.** People trust leaders who remain calm when circumstances are chaotic.
- **It inspires courage.** Teams draw strength when their leader demonstrates composure and conviction.
- **It defines culture.** Repeated patterns of resilience embed courage, adaptability, and hope into organizational identity.
- **It endures in memory.** Years later, people rarely recall quarterly results but vividly remember whether their leader led with fear or faithfulness.

For Leaders at All Levels:
- A **supervisor** builds legacy by standing with their team through stressful workloads instead of withdrawing into self-preservation.
- A **manager** builds legacy by staying calm and transparent when goals shift, helping their team reframe challenges as opportunities.
- An **executive** builds legacy by leading an organization through turbulence with clarity, values, and humanity, setting a cultural tone that will last long after their tenure.

Holistic leaders understand this truth: storms are temporary, but the memory of how you led through them is permanent. Resilience is not only about surviving adversity—it is about shaping a story of courage and steadiness that will be remembered by those who follow. A resilient leader's legacy is not written in avoidance of hardship but in the way they transformed hardship into hope. Legacy isn't survival—it's steadiness remembered.

From Theory to Practice

Resilience is not an abstract idea or a leadership slogan; it is a daily discipline. Leaders do not become resilient in the moment of crisis—they reveal the resilience they have built over time. The storms of leadership expose whether we have cultivated habits that sustain us or whether we have drifted into patterns that collapse under pressure.

Resilience becomes real when it is practiced consistently in small ways, long before the big tests arrive. Every meeting, every decision, and every response to stress is an opportunity to strengthen or weaken resilience. Over time, these daily practices form the muscle memory that leaders and teams draw on when adversity strikes.

Five Habits of Resilient Leaders
1. **Pause Before Reacting:** Resilient leaders resist the urge to react impulsively under pressure. They create space to breathe, reflect, and respond thoughtfully. Even a brief pause can prevent rash words or hasty decisions that add to chaos.

2. **Name Challenges Honestly:** Spin may protect image, but it weakens trust. Resilient leaders acknowledge reality while framing it with hope: *"This is difficult, but we will face it together."* Honesty validates the struggle; hope inspires perseverance.
3. **Practice Renewal Daily:** Renewal is not an occasional retreat; it is a rhythm. Resilient leaders guard their energy by prioritizing rest, reflection, and healthy boundaries. By doing so, they model sustainability and give others permission to do the same.
4. **Celebrate Progress:** Motivation wanes when teams feel like they are endlessly climbing without rest. Resilient leaders sustain energy by celebrating small wins along the way. Recognition reminds people that their effort matters and that progress is being made, even if the finish line is distant.
5. **Anchor in Legacy:** Resilience is strengthened when leaders connect present struggles to future impact. Adversity becomes more bearable when people understand that it is shaping them into the kind of leaders they hope to be. Resilient leaders remind themselves and their teams that storms refine character and forge legacy.

I often tell teams, *"Our legacy isn't written when everything is smooth. It's written in how we respond when things are hard."* Smooth seasons reveal little about leadership, but storms reveal everything. By practicing these habits daily, leaders ensure that when storms come, they are not unprepared—they are anchored, steady, and able to lead others with courage and renewal.

Pitfalls and Best Practices
Pitfall 1: Ignoring Burnout
- Example: Pushing teams harder without acknowledging limits.
- Best Practice: Name fatigue, then build space for renewal.

Pitfall 2: Overconfidence in Crisis
- Example: Pretending everything is fine to avoid showing weakness.
- Best Practice: Model vulnerability while providing direction.

Pitfall 3: Equating Resilience with Toughness
- Example: Rewarding overwork instead of sustainable effort.
- Best Practice: Celebrate perseverance paired with healthy renewal.

Pitfall 4: Neglecting Renewal
- Example: Leading teams through a challenge but never creating space for recovery.
- Best Practice: Build rhythms of rest, reflection, and celebration into the culture.

Reflective Questions
1. How do you personally practice renewal in seasons of challenge?
2. What signals show that your team is experiencing fatigue or burnout?
3. How do you help others reframe obstacles into opportunities?
4. What practices keep you anchored in purpose during adversity?
5. How will your response to hardship shape your leadership legacy?
6. Which storm most shaped your leadership character?

Journaling Prompts
- Write about a time you faced adversity and found strength you didn't know you had.
- Reflect on how your leadership response to difficulty shaped your team's trust.
- Journal about one renewal practice you want to strengthen this month.
- Describe the legacy you want to leave in how you respond to adversity.

90-Day Resilience and Renewal Plan

Month 1 – Personal Resilience
- Begin daily journaling on challenges and lessons.
- Set one non-negotiable boundary to protect rest and energy.

Month 2 – Team Resilience
- Hold a reflection session on a recent challenge.
- Normalize conversations about stress and energy in meetings.
- Celebrate one small team milestone.

Month 3 – Embedding Renewal
- Introduce a renewal practice into team culture (gratitude ritual, reflection time, celebration).
- Share a personal resilience practice with your team as a model.
- Reconnect the team to purpose by asking: *"Why does this work matter?"*

By the end of 90 days, you will not only strengthen your own resilience but also embed rhythms of renewal in your team, shaping a culture that faces adversity with courage and carries resilience as part of its legacy.

Resilient leaders endure, and renewing leaders sustain. Together, these qualities shape a legacy of courage and steadiness. People will remember not only that you faced adversity but how you faced it — with integrity, with hope, and with the capacity to rise again.

10 THE POWER OF LEGACY AND LASTING IMPACT

Leadership is temporary, but legacy endures. Titles pass, positions shift, results fade, but the imprint of your leadership continues in the people you shaped, the culture you built, and the values you lived. Legacy is leadership's ultimate measure.

When I think about leadership, I no longer measure it only by today's successes. I ask myself: *What will remain when I'm no longer in the room? What will people carry forward because of the seeds I've planted?* For me, that is legacy.

I speak often about what I want my own legacy to be — not just systems or programs, but people. I want to leave behind leaders who are stronger, more courageous, and more principled because of the time we spent together. I want those I've invested in to lead others with confidence and conviction, multiplying the impact long after I am gone. That is what guides my choices. Every decision, every conversation, every investment of energy is measured not only by its immediate outcome but by the future it creates.

Legacy is not what we leave behind by accident; it is what we build on purpose. That is the heart of legacy: choosing today what will matter tomorrow.

Holistic Leadership and Legacy

Throughout this book, we have explored holistic leadership — leadership that integrates vision and values, courage and compassion, strategy and character. At its core, holistic leadership is not about excelling in one dimension of influence but about weaving all dimensions together into a life of integrity and impact. Legacy is the natural outflow of this integration.

A leader who is strategic but not ethical may achieve results but will struggle to be remembered with honor. A leader who inspires but never develops others may shine for a moment but leave no successors to carry the work forward. A leader who perseveres through adversity but neglects renewal may endure for a time but fade without sustaining influence. Holistic leadership brings these pieces together so that legacy is whole, not fragmented.

Why Holistic Leadership Creates Lasting Legacy

- **Integration of Values and Vision:** Legacy is durable when values undergird vision, ensuring that what is built reflects integrity.
- **Investment in People:** Legacy multiplies when leaders see people not as means to an end but as the end itself.
- **Balance of Resilience and Renewal:** Legacy is sustained when leaders endure storms without burning out, modeling rhythms of hope.
- **Commitment to Innovation Anchored in Purpose:** Legacy grows when leaders dare to imagine the future but keep creativity tethered to mission.

Holistic leaders measure success by the imprint they leave on people, cultures, and futures. Their legacy is not piecemeal but complete — the sum of vision, character, and influence practiced consistently over time.

When leadership is holistic, legacy is inevitable. It is written not only in achievements but in the lives touched, the values embodied, and the futures imagined. Holistic leadership ensures that what endures is not just what you accomplished, but who you became and who you empowered others to become.

The Dimensions of Legacy

Legacy is not one-dimensional; it is the sum of many layers of influence. A leader's impact extends far beyond projects and results — it is carried in the lives, systems, and values they leave behind. Holistic leaders recognize that a lasting legacy emerges in at least three dimensions:

1. Personal Legacy – Who You Were

At the core of legacy is character. People may forget the exact goals you reached, but they will not forget how you carried yourself in moments of pressure, conflict, or decision. Personal legacy is the imprint of integrity, humility, and courage. It is built when leaders live consistently in public and private, when their words and actions align. The memory of your leadership will rest as much in *who you were* as in *what you accomplished*.

2. Relational Legacy – How You Treated People

Leadership is always relational. Long after metrics fade, people will remember how you made them feel: valued, overlooked, empowered, or dismissed. Relational legacy is carried in the encouragement you gave, the trust you built, and the leaders you developed. It is found in the mentee who still remembers your affirmation years later, or the colleague who learned resilience because of your support. This dimension reminds us that people are not stepping stones to legacy — they *are* the legacy.

3. Institutional Legacy – What You Built

Legacy is also carried in the cultures, systems, and structures you helped shape. Did you build an environment where values are embedded into daily practice? Did you design systems that continue to serve people long after you are gone? Institutional legacy ensures that leadership is not dependent on one person's presence but embedded in the DNA of an organization or community. Cultures outlast titles, and healthy systems extend influence far beyond one leader's season.

Living in All Three Dimensions

Holistic leaders do not focus on one dimension at the expense of the others. Personal integrity without people development leaves an incomplete imprint. Strong relationships without systems for continuity may fade when the leader departs. Durable legacy is built when who you are, how you treat people, and what you create all reinforce one another.

When you reflect on your own legacy, ask yourself:
- *What values will define me when I'm remembered?*
- *How will people describe the way I treated them?*
- *What practices or cultures will endure because of me?*

Legacy is the sum of these dimensions woven together. And the leaders remembered most are those whose lives were consistent across all three. Durable legacy grows where integrity, relationships, and systems reinforce one another.

Frameworks for Legacy-Minded Leadership

Legacy is not built on good intentions alone. It requires structures, tools, and rhythms that help leaders translate values into consistent action. Without intentional frameworks, even the best aspirations risk being lost in the noise of urgent demands. Frameworks give legacy shape — they provide practical ways to reflect, align, and act so that influence endures. What follows are guiding tools that help leaders move from abstract ideals to lived practices of legacy-minded leadership.

The Legacy Map

The Legacy Map invites leaders to think intentionally about their influence in three circles: *Self, People, and Impact*. In the *Self* circle, leaders reflect on the values they refused to compromise. These are the non-negotiables that define their integrity—moments when they chose principle over convenience. In the *People* circle, leaders consider those they invested in: the colleagues, protégés, or community members whose growth they nurtured. Finally, in the *Impact* circle, leaders identify the practices, systems, or cultural shifts they helped embed that will endure long after they are gone. The Legacy Map offers leaders a profound but straightforward tool for reflection on Self, People, and Impact.

Daily Legacy Alignment

Legacy is not only built in milestones; it is forged in daily habits. A simple rhythm of *morning intention, values-based decision-making, and evening reflection* keeps leaders aligned with their deeper purpose. Each morning, leaders set intention by asking, *"How do I want my leadership to be remembered today?"*

During the day, they run decisions through a values filter, resisting expedient shortcuts that undermine trust. At day's end, they reflect: *"Did I live true to my commitments today? Where did I fall short, and how can I reset tomorrow?"*

This discipline transforms legacy from an abstract concept into a lived practice. Over time, these daily alignments compound, creating consistency that followers come to trust. The result is not perfection but authenticity—leaders remembered for being the same in private as in public.

Succession Thinking

Legacy-minded leaders measure success not by how indispensable they are, but by how well others thrive after them. Succession thinking shifts focus from personal performance to preparing others to carry the vision forward. It asks: *"Who am I developing to lead when I am gone?"* This does not only apply to top roles; it extends to every level where influence matters.

Succession thinking involves mentoring, coaching, and providing opportunities for stretch assignments that prepare others for greater responsibility. Leaders who adopt this mindset resist the temptation of hoarding power. Instead, they create multiplying leaders who sustain and expand impact. A true legacy is not when people say, *"We could not go on without them,"* but when they say, *"Because of them, we are ready for what's next."*

Cultural Embedding

Cultures are shaped less by what leaders declare and more by what they consistently reinforce. Legacy-minded leaders embed values into the very fabric of their organizations through *stories, rituals, and recognition*. Stories retold in meetings or onboarding sessions remind people of defining moments when values were lived out. Rituals—whether annual service days, opening team meetings with gratitude, or celebrating milestones—normalize values as part of daily rhythm. Recognition, both formal and informal, highlights those who embody the culture, reinforcing what matters most.

Cultural embedding ensures that values are not dependent on a single leader's presence. They become part of "how we do things here," providing continuity long after leaders transition. The culture itself becomes the carrier of legacy.

The Legacy Question

Perhaps the most powerful framework is also the simplest: *"What will endure because of this choice?"* This question reframes decisions in the light of permanence. It challenges leaders to move beyond short-term wins, asking whether the ripple effects of today's actions will still be meaningful tomorrow, next year, or even in the next generation.

Leaders who live by the Legacy Question avoid the trap of chasing recognition or immediate results at the expense of trust and impact. Instead, they choose what will stand the test of time. By making this question part of their leadership reflex, they ensure that their influence leaves more than footprints in the sand—it leaves foundations on which others can build.

Personal Influence That Outlasts the Moment

I remember walking into a room months after a project had ended and overhearing a team referencing a phrase I had repeated often during our work together. It had become part of their language, a shorthand for how they approached challenges. That was legacy in its simplest form — not my presence, but my influence, continuing to shape how they worked and thought.

Moments like these remind me that legacy is less about position and more about presence. It is not what leaders hold but what they release into others that matters most.

The Interwoven Threads of Leadership and Legacy

Throughout this journey, we've explored practices that, when woven together, create a legacy of holistic leadership:

- Casting a **vision** that inspires people to lift their eyes beyond today.
- Practicing **self-awareness** and emotional intelligence so our influence builds trust.
- Leading with **communication and courage**, creating space for dialogue even in conflict.
- Grounding leadership in **character and virtue**, making choices that align with our values.
- Investing in others through **coaching and mentorship**, multiplying leadership at every level.
- Choosing **ethics and moral courage** when compromise would be easier.
- Practicing **resilience and renewal** through adversity, modeling steadiness and hope.

All of these threads together form the fabric of legacy. Legacy is not a single act or decision. It is the accumulation of choices that reflect who we are and what we value most.

Practical Frameworks for Building Legacy

Legacy can feel abstract unless leaders anchor it in rhythms and tools that make it tangible. The most effective leaders don't simply hope to leave a legacy — they practice it daily. Practical frameworks provide a way to translate lofty intentions into everyday action.

The Legacy Map

The Legacy Map, introduced earlier, offers leaders a simple but profound tool for reflection. By visualizing three concentric circles, leaders can regularly assess how they are shaping legacy at different levels:

- **Inner Circle (Self):** Who am I becoming as a leader? What values define me? This circle is about identity and integrity. Legacy starts with the kind of person you choose to be when no one is watching. Are you consistent? Do your private decisions match your public words? The strongest legacies begin with alignment between character and action.
- **Middle Circle (People):** Who am I developing? How am I investing in others? This circle represents relationships and influence. Legacy multiplies when leaders intentionally mentor, coach, and empower others. Who are you pouring into today that will lead tomorrow?
- **Outer Circle (Impact):** What am I building that will outlast me? This circle focuses on culture and systems. Are you embedding values into structures, rituals, and practices that will endure? The outer circle ensures your legacy is not dependent on presence alone but on systems that reinforce what you stood for.

Leaders can revisit this map weekly, monthly, or quarterly, asking: *Am I aligned with the legacy I want to leave? Where am I strong? Where do I need to grow?* Over time, this practice sharpens clarity and reinforces intentionality.

Daily Alignment Practices

Legacy is not only built in milestones; it is forged in daily habits. These practices serve as anchors for leaders who want to ensure their daily actions match their long-term vision:

1. **Morning Intention:** Begin each day with one question: *What can I do today that aligns with my legacy?* This frames the day not around tasks alone but around impact.
2. **Values Filter:** Run major decisions through your values. If they contradict, adjust course — even when it costs more time or energy. This filter prevents drift from principle into expedience.
3. **Leadership Deposits:** Treat every interaction as a chance to plant seeds of encouragement, growth, or vision. Even small conversations can leave lasting imprints. Ask yourself: *What deposit am I making in this person today?*
4. **End-of-Day Reflection:** Close the day by journaling on how your actions moved you closer to the legacy you intend. Reflection turns experience into learning and ensures progress is not left to chance.

Why These Practices Matter

When leaders pair tools like the Legacy Map with daily alignment habits, legacy ceases to be abstract. It becomes a lived reality, built choice by choice. These frameworks also keep leaders humble and accountable: legacy is not a single achievement but the consistency of thousands of small actions.

Holistic leaders understand this truth: legacy is shaped as much in the unnoticed, ordinary rhythms as in the extraordinary moments. By practicing intentional alignment daily, leaders ensure that the story being written about their leadership is not left to chance but guided by conviction.

The Price of Legacy

Every leader desires to leave a lasting mark, but few fully embrace the cost that legacy requires. Legacy is not built on convenience; it is forged in sacrifice. It asks leaders to give more than they take, to plant seeds that may not bloom during their tenure, and to invest in people and values even when recognition never comes.

The Sacrifice of Time
Legacy requires time — time to listen when it would be faster to decide, time to mentor when deadlines press in, time to reflect when urgency screams for action. Leaders often underestimate how much of legacy is shaped in unglamorous moments: the one-on-one conversation that boosts confidence, the feedback session that turns potential into growth, the pause to explain not just the *what* but the *why*.

The Sacrifice of Recognition
Much of legacy work is invisible. Systems that function smoothly, cultures that live out values, and leaders who rise to take your place rarely carry your name. Legacy is costly because it often requires letting go of immediate credit in order to secure long-term impact. Legacy-minded leaders trade applause today for influence tomorrow.

The Sacrifice of Comfort
Legacy also costs comfort. Upholding values in moments of pressure, choosing people over expedience, or daring to innovate when it would be safer to maintain the status quo — all these choices stretch leaders beyond convenience. True legacy asks, *What will endure because of this choice?* even when that choice comes at a personal price.

The Sacrifice of Control
Finally, legacy costs control. Leaders who cling to indispensability choke their influence. Those who release power, delegate authority, and prepare others to lead extend their legacy beyond themselves. Succession thinking is humbling: it means acknowledging that the work will go on without you — and that this is a sign of success, not failure.

Why the Cost Is Worth It
Legacy costs more than immediate results, but it delivers more than immediate rewards. The leaders remembered most are not those who protected comfort or clung to recognition, but those who sacrificed for something greater than themselves. Legacy is built in the moments when leaders choose investment over indulgence, principle over popularity, and future impact over present ease.

Holistic leaders understand this truth: legacy demands sacrifice, but it also multiplies influence. What feels costly today becomes priceless tomorrow when people carry forward your values, your culture, and your vision. The question is not whether legacy will cost you, but whether you are willing to pay that cost for an impact that will endure beyond your lifetime.

Succession and Continuity

Legacy is not only about personal impact; it is also about ensuring continuity through others. A leader's influence is proven not when everything depends on them, but when the work continues — and even thrives — in their absence. Legacy-minded leaders think in terms of succession. They prepare others not only to maintain what exists but to carry it further, adapting and strengthening it for a new season.

Why Succession Matters

Too often, leaders fall into the trap of equating indispensability with importance. They measure their worth by how much the organization "needs" them. But true legacy is not when people say, *"We could not go on without them."* It is when people say, *"Because of them, we are ready for what's next."* Succession ensures that influence multiplies, rather than ends, when the leader departs.

Building Continuity Through People

Succession begins by identifying and developing future leaders at every level:

- A **supervisor** might teach a team member to run meetings, preparing them for leadership opportunities.
- A **manager** might delegate a project to a rising star, allowing them to build confidence and competence.
- An **executive** might design pipelines for talent development, ensuring that leadership readiness becomes part of organizational culture.

In each case, the focus shifts from holding power to releasing it. Leaders who practice succession are not diminished — they are multiplied.

Building Continuity Through Culture

Systems and values are just as critical as people. Leaders must embed their values into rituals, language, and processes so that even as people transition, the culture continues to reflect what they stood for. For example:

- Embedding storytelling into onboarding to preserve defining moments of culture.
- Creating rituals of recognition that reinforce core values.
- Documenting processes not only for efficiency but for alignment with mission.

When culture is codified and reinforced, it becomes the invisible thread of continuity, ensuring the organization does not lose its way when leaders change. Succession is generosity in motion—leadership that lets go so others can rise.

The Succession Question

Every leader should regularly ask:

- *If I left tomorrow, what would remain?*
- *What would disappear?*
- *What do I need to build today to ensure continuity tomorrow?*

The answers to these questions reveal whether legacy is being built on personality alone or on principles that can endure.

Succession as a Gift, Not a Threat

Some leaders fear succession because it feels like replacement. But succession is not about erasing influence — it is about extending it. By preparing others, leaders ensure their values live on. It is an act of generosity, not loss. Leaders who invest in succession give their organizations, families, and communities the gift of stability and growth long after they are gone.

Holistic leaders understand this: legacy is not about being remembered for holding on tightly but for passing on wisely. Continuity is the true measure of leadership's depth. The seeds of legacy do not wither when leaders transition; they take root in the lives and systems left behind, continuing to grow into futures the leader may never see.

Legacy as Multiplication

True legacy is not measured by how much one leader accomplishes alone but by how much they multiply in others. Addition is when a leader's influence grows through their own effort; multiplication is when that influence expands exponentially because they developed others who continue the work. Legacy-minded leaders understand that their greatest impact will not be in what they personally achieve, but in the leaders they inspire, equip, and release. Legacy expands exponentially when leadership is shared.

Addition vs. Multiplication

- **Addition:** You achieve goals, complete projects, and accumulate results. These are good, but they end with you.
- **Multiplication:** You raise up others who achieve goals, complete projects, and influence still more people. These results outlast you and ripple outward in ways you may never fully see.

Why Multiplication Matters

A leader who completes ten projects has influence for a season. A leader who equips ten people to lead can influence thousands across generations. Multiplication ensures that vision is not dependent on one individual's energy or presence but becomes a shared movement carried forward by many.

For Leaders at All Levels:

- A **supervisor** multiplies legacy when they train team members to lead shifts confidently in their absence.
- A **manager** multiplies legacy when they develop a culture of mentorship, so growth becomes everyone's responsibility.
- An **executive** multiplies legacy when they build systems and pipelines that prepare future leaders for the organization's highest roles.

The Multiplication Mindset

Leaders who embrace multiplication stop asking, *"What can I accomplish?"* and start asking, *"Who can I develop?"* They measure success not by how indispensable they are but by how prepared others are to thrive without them. Multiplication requires humility, patience, and the willingness to release authority — but it also delivers the most enduring legacy.

Holistic leaders understand this: legacy grows when influence is shared. A leader who multiplies leaders ensures that their values, vision, and culture continue to spread long after they are gone. Multiplication is the key to turning leadership influence into generational impact.

Stories That Carry Legacy

Every leader writes stories into the lives of others. Some of those stories will be remembered and retold for years; others will live quietly in the habits, choices, and words people carry forward. Legacy is less about what leaders say about themselves and more about the stories others will tell about them.

Cultures are built on stories. Families retell defining moments. Organizations share anecdotes about their founders or pivotal seasons. Communities rally around stories of courage, sacrifice, and vision. As leaders, the way you show up in moments of tension, opportunity, or failure becomes the material others use to describe your influence.

Some stories are dramatic — the bold decision to protect values in the face of pressure, the vision that changed the trajectory of a team, the act of courage that defined a season. But many stories are ordinary:

- The moment you remembered someone's name when they felt unseen.
- The encouragement you gave that became someone's turning point.
- The consistency you modeled when others wavered. These small stories often outlast the headlines. They are repeated not because they were grand, but because they were true.

The Responsibility of Story-Shaping

Every leader should ask: *What stories will people tell about me?* Will they describe a leader who inspired fear or one who cultivated courage? Will they remember someone who hoarded credit or someone who freely gave recognition? Will they recall pressure without compassion, or resilience anchored in hope?

For Leaders at All Levels
- A **supervisor** leaves stories when they defend their team against unfair criticism.
- A **manager** leaves stories when they empower someone to take a risk that changes their career.
- An **executive** leaves stories when they choose principle over profit, shaping organizational identity for years to come.

Living as a Story Worth Retelling
Legacy is not just the formal record of your achievements but the informal stories others pass along. These stories ripple outward, shaping how people think, speak, and act long after you are gone. The challenge for every leader is to live in such a way that the stories people tell about you reflect courage, integrity, and hope.

Holistic leaders understand this: the most enduring legacies are not written in reports or plaques, but in the stories others choose to retell. And the story of your leadership is being written right now — one decision, one interaction, one moment at a time.

Legacy in Action: Small Moments, Lasting Impact
Legacies are often forged in moments that seem ordinary at the time. A word of encouragement that becomes someone's anchor. A difficult decision that reinforces values. A risk taken that inspires courage in others. These choices ripple outward, shaping people and culture in ways leaders may never fully see.

One of the most humbling parts of leadership is realizing that you may never witness the full extent of your influence. But that is the beauty of legacy — it multiplies quietly, invisibly, carried forward in the lives of those you've touched. Legacy is most often revealed in moments you cannot control — when others repeat your words, model your values, or continue your work without your presence. That is when you know your leadership has multiplied. Legacy often reveals itself in echoes, not applause.

From Theory to Practice
Legacy is not accidental. It does not emerge only at retirement parties or in the memories of others after you are gone. Legacy is built, brick by brick, in the daily choices of a leader. Intentionality is what transforms ordinary actions into lasting influence. When leaders commit to living with legacy in mind each day, they ensure that their imprint is not left to chance but shaped by design.

Five Daily Habits of Legacy-Minded Leaders
1. **Live Your Values Consistently**
   Integrity is the foundation of legacy. Followers quickly notice gaps between what leaders say and what they do. When values are compromised in small ways, credibility erodes in large ways. Legacy is built when leaders are the same person in private as they are in public, when their decisions reflect principles even under pressure.
   - *Example:* A supervisor refuses to cut corners on safety to save time. A manager communicates transparently about challenges rather than softening the truth. These consistent choices, though costly in the moment, build trust that lasts far longer than the results themselves.
2. **Invest in Others Regularly**
   Legacy is multiplied through people. Developing at least one person intentionally ensures that your leadership does not end with you. This habit may take the form of mentoring, coaching, or simply creating opportunities for others to lead. Over time, the people you invest in will become carriers of your influence.
   - *Example:* A leader sets aside 30 minutes each week to meet with an emerging team member, offering feedback, encouragement, and perspective. The consistency communicates that people, not just tasks, are the priority.
3. **Anchor in Purpose**
   Projects and goals will fade, but purpose endures. Legacy-minded leaders ensure that every initiative connects back to a larger mission. This anchoring prevents teams from losing sight of why their work matters and ensures that energy is directed toward what will outlast the moment.
   - *Example:* Before launching a new program, a leader asks, *"How does this align with our mission and values?"* This simple filter prevents drift and keeps efforts tied to long-term impact.

4. **Communicate Vision Often**
   Legacy is sustained when vision becomes culture. Leaders must repeat the "why" consistently until it becomes part of how people think and speak. Vision casting is not a one-time speech; it is an ongoing rhythm of reminding people where they are headed and why it matters.
   - *Example:* A manager begins each staff meeting by connecting the week's tasks back to the organization's larger goals. An executive weaves vision into every presentation, ensuring that strategy is always tied to purpose.

5. **Think Beyond Self**
   Legacy grows when leaders move from self-preservation to self-giving. This habit requires asking: *"How will this decision affect people and culture long after I'm gone?"* Legacy-minded leaders resist the temptation to build their own name and instead build futures that others can inherit.
   - *Example:* A leader chooses to document processes and share knowledge rather than keeping it to themselves. In doing so, they ensure continuity, showing that true leadership is about release, not retention.

Why These Habits Matter

Practicing these habits daily keeps legacy from becoming an abstract ideal and turns it into a lived reality. They are simple, but their cumulative effect is profound. Over weeks, months, and years, they shape a consistent pattern of influence that followers come to rely on and remember.

Holistic leaders understand this truth: legacy is not built at the end of the journey but in the steps taken every day. The question is never *if* you are leaving a legacy, but *what kind* of legacy you are shaping through your habits right now.

Pitfalls and Best Practices in Legacy

Pitfall 1: Chasing Titles and Recognition
- *Danger:* Legacy becomes confused with fame.
- *Best Practice:* Focus on impact, not image. Titles fade; influence remains.

Pitfall 2: Prioritizing Short-Term Wins
- *Danger:* Achievements may look impressive, but leave no lasting value.
- *Best Practice:* Anchor every project to a long-term purpose.

Pitfall 3: Ignoring People Development
- *Danger:* Systems survive, but people stagnate.
- *Best Practice:* Invest in developing others as much as achieving goals.

Pitfall 4: Leaving Without Continuity
- *Danger:* A vision dies when the leader departs.
- *Best Practice:* Build succession plans and embed values in culture.

Reflective Questions
1. What three words do you want people to use when they describe your leadership legacy?
2. How do your daily decisions reflect or contradict that legacy?
3. Who are you developing to carry forward your influence?
4. What systems or practices would remain if you stepped away today?
5. How will your leadership shape the culture long after you are gone?

Journaling Prompts
- Write about one moment when you saw your leadership ripple beyond your presence.
- Journal about the legacy someone else left in your life and how it shaped you.
- Reflect on how each theme in this book contributes to your own leadership legacy.
- Describe one legacy-building practice you will begin this month to align with your intended legacy.

90-Day Legacy Plan

Month 1 – Clarify Your Legacy
- Write your personal leadership legacy statement.
- Share it with someone you trust for accountability.

Month 2 – Align Your Actions
- Audit your calendar: Does your time reflect your stated legacy?
- Make one intentional adjustment to bring greater alignment.

Month 3 – Multiply Your Influence
- Identify and invest in at least one emerging leader.
- Share your values and vision with your team.
- Document one system or process that embeds your leadership into culture.

By the end of 90 days, you will not only have clarified your legacy but begun to live it daily, building momentum that extends far beyond your presence.

A Final Word: Your Legacy Starts Now

As I bring this book to a close, I want to speak to you directly. Everything you've read here — every story, every framework, every principle — has been building toward one truth: leadership is not about today alone. It is about the imprint you will leave tomorrow. Titles will change, roles will shift, results will fade, but the influence you carry into people, cultures, and values will continue. That is the essence of legacy.

You don't have to wait until retirement, until you achieve a certain position, or until you feel "ready" to begin shaping your legacy. It begins now, in the ordinary choices you make each day. It is present in the way you greet your team in the morning, the honesty with which you handle conflict, the vision you cast for the future, and the courage you show when compromise would be easier. Every action is a seed. Some will bloom quickly, others may take years, but each one has the potential to grow into something that outlasts you.

Legacy is not a distant horizon — it is a present reality. The way you lead *today* is writing the story others will tell *tomorrow*. The question is not whether you will leave a legacy, but what kind of legacy you will leave. Will it be one of integrity, courage, and hope? Or one of expedience, fear, and self-preservation? That choice belongs to you, every single day.

My challenge to you is this: don't just lead — lead with legacy in mind. Lead with the awareness that every meeting, every decision, every word spoken plants something in the lives of others. Build not only for success but for significance. Measure not only what you accomplish but who you develop. Dare not only to imagine the future but to prepare others to carry it forward.

Live with intention. Lead with courage. Build with hope. And remember that your leadership is more than a role; it is a gift — a gift entrusted to you not for your own sake but for the generations that follow. Legacy is not about someday; it is about today. The story of your leadership is being written now, one choice at a time.

So write it well. Live it fully. Lead it faithfully. And let your legacy be one that endures.

Your legacy starts now.

REFERENCES

Bridges, W. (2009). *Managing Transitions: Making the Most of Change.* Da Capo Press.
Duckworth, A. (2016). *Grit: The Power of Passion and Perseverance.* Scribner.
Edmondson, A. C. (2019). *The Fearless Organization: Creating Psychological Safety in the Workplace for Learning, Innovation, and Growth.* Wiley.
Gallup. (2001). *Now, Discover Your Strengths.* Free Press.
Heifetz, R., & Linsky, M. (2002). *Leadership on the Line: Staying Alive Through the Dangers of Leading.* Harvard Business Review Press.
Kim, W. C., & Mauborgne, R. (2005). *Blue Ocean Strategy: How to Create Uncontested Market Space and Make the Competition Irrelevant.* Harvard Business Review Press.
Kotter, J. P. (1996). *Leading Change.* Harvard Business School Press.
Prosci. (2018). *ADKAR: A Model for Change in Business, Government, and Our Community.* Prosci Learning Center Publications.
Rath, T., & Conchie, B. (2008). *Strengths-Based Leadership: Great Leaders, Teams, and Why People Follow.* Gallup Press.
Rosenberg, M. B. (2015). *Nonviolent Communication: A Language of Life.* PuddleDancer Press.
Thomas, K. W., & Kilmann, R. H. (1974). *Thomas-Kilmann Conflict Mode Instrument.* Xicom.
Tuckman, B. W. (1965). "Developmental Sequence in Small Groups." *Psychological Bulletin,* 63(6), 384–399.
Stanford d.school. (2010). *An Introduction to Design Thinking: Process Guide.* Hasso Plattner Institute of Design at Stanford.
The Predictive Index. (n.d.). *The Predictive Index Behavioral Assessment.* Retrieved from https://www.predictiveindex.com.

ABOUT THE AUTHOR

Dr. Jamika L. Bivens is a leadership strategist, educator, and developer of people who has dedicated her career to shaping leaders who inspire lasting impact. She designs and leads initiatives that strengthen organizational culture, build high-performing teams, and prepare the next generation of leaders.

With a background that blends academic rigor and practical experience, Bivens brings a holistic perspective to leadership—one that integrates vision, character, communication, resilience, and innovation. She has earned recognition for her ability to translate complex frameworks into actionable practices that transform both individuals and organizations.

Beyond her professional achievements, Bivens is passionate about mentoring, community service, and equipping others to discover their unique leadership voice. She believes leadership is not measured by titles or accolades but by the legacy we leave in people, culture, and values.

The Power of Legacy: Holistic Leadership for Lasting Impact is both her vision and her invitation—to leaders at every level—to embrace a way of leading that is purposeful, courageous, and enduring.

www.ingramcontent.com/pod-product-compliance
Lightning Source LLC
LaVergne TN
LVHW022232080526
838199LV00105B/265